OUR
FIERY TRIAL

ABRAHAM LINCOLN,
JOHN BROWN,
AND
THE CIVIL WAR ERA

STEPHEN B. OATES

University of Massachusetts Press

Amherst, 1979

Copyright © 1979 by The University of Massachusetts Press
Library of Congress Catalog Card Number 78–16286
ISBN 0–87023–397–1
Printed in the United States of America
Designed by Mary Mendell
Library of Congress Cataloging in Publication Data
Oates, Stephen B
Our fiery trial.
Bibliography: p.
Includes index.
1. Lincoln, Abraham, Pres. U.S., 1809–1865—
Addresses, essays, lectures. 2. Brown, John, 1800–
1859—Addresses, essays, lectures. 3. Turner, Nat,
1800?–1831—Addresses, essays, lectures. 4. United
States—History—Civil War, 1861–1865—Addresses,
essays, lectures. I. Title.
E457.8.O18   973.7   78–16286

"Styron's War against the Blacks" first appeared under the title, "Styron and the Blacks —Another View," in *The Nation* 220 (May 1975). "John Brown and His Judges" first appeared in *Civil War History* 17 (March 1971). "Modern Radicals and John Brown" first appeared under the title " 'In Thine Own Image': Modern Radicals and John Brown," in the *South Atlantic Quarterly* 73 (Autumn, 1974). Copyright 1974 by Duke University Press. "The Enigma of Stephen A. Douglas" first appeared under the title "The Little Giant Reconsidered," in *Reviews in American History* (December 1973). Reprinted with permission. "Ghost Riders in the Sky" first appeared in *The Colorado Quarterly* 23 (Summer 1974).

For
David D. Van Tassel

CONTENTS

T

HE studies gathered here focus on the Age of the Civil War and some of the leading personae in the tragedy of that conflict—among them, Abraham Lincoln, John Brown, Nat Turner, Stephen A. Douglas, and the Southern secessionists. On one level, this serves as a companion volume to my biographical trilogy—*The Fires of Jubilee: Nat Turner's Fierce Rebellion, To Purge This Land with Blood: A Biography of John Brown,* and *With Malice toward None: The Life of Abraham Lincoln.* Several of the essays, in fact, grew out of the reading and research I did for the trilogy. Among other things, they examine some of the literary and historical controversies that surround the three men and their era, try to clarify my ideas about them and add new insights, and generally pursue topics I thought more appropriate for essays than for biographies.

"God's Stone in the Pool of Slavery," for example, analyzes Harpers Ferry in the context of Southern anxieties and apprehensions over slavery that had been growing since the beginning of the Republic—and especially since Nat Turner's rebellion. The essay demonstrates that on one score John Brown proved himself a keenly perceptive man, for he correctly predicted the explosive impact his raid would have on Southern whites. For them, Harpers Ferry was no isolated outbreak of little historical import. It was instead an apocalyptic outgrowth of Northern antislavery agitation, an act of "outside provocation" that caused white Southerners to equate Brown-style revolutionary violence with Lincoln and the Republican party and that escalated sectional tensions over slavery to the breaking point. In this respect, *Our Fiery Trial* shows

how symbolically significant Turner, Brown, and Lincoln were in
Southern eyes, how profoundly interconnected they were in the
whirlwind of events that spun the United States toward civil
war, how inextricably bound up all three were in the haunting
problem of slavery in their day.

"Lincoln's Journey to Emancipation," for its part, challenges
two widely accepted interpretations about Lincoln's Emancipation
Proclamation and his views on race. The first interpretation, pop-
ularized by Richard Hofstadter, argues that the Proclamation went
no further than the Second Confiscation Act and that it did not
in fact liberate any slaves. Furthermore, Hofstadter thought it represented the sentiments of the average Northerner of the time,
proving that in the matter of emancipation Lincoln was a follower
and not a leader of public opinion. The second interpretation,
advanced by George M. Fredrickson, contends that Lincoln remained to the end of his life a paternalist in race relations and
a diehard champion of colonization. This book not only disputes
both of these views, but also points out that at war's end the
president was considering a tougher Reconstruction policy than
most Lincoln biographers and Civil War historians have claimed.

Another essay, "The Enigma of Stephen A. Douglas," offers a
critical re-evaluation of Lincoln's arch rival and reviews the major
writings about that stormy and inconsistent man. "The Long
Shadow of Lincoln" is an *explication de text* of three major Lincoln source books—and three views of Lincoln himself—and a
celebration, too, of the enduring literary and historical value of
authentic contemporary accounts. And "Themes and Variations
of a Civil War Trilogy," which serves as an epilogue to the book,
is both a discussion of the nature and purpose of my three intersecting "lives" and an ode to biography as a literary art.

On another level, this book transcends the Civil War era and
reflects some of my more universal concerns as a biographer and
a humanist: the role of people in shaping the course of events, the
subjective nature of historical interpretation, the purpose of true
biography, and the abuses of the past by poets, modern novelists,
political advocates, and professional historians themselves. In particular, I have explored how both William Styron and politicized
blacks have misused Nat Turner and in the process have generated
two vitally important questions: How much license does a fiction-
ist have in changing historical situations and altering actual his-

torical figures to suit the dictates of his story? Moreover, what
happens to the truths of history when it becomes a mouthpiece
for modern politics? Two companion essays, "John Brown and His
Judges" and "Modern Radicals and John Brown," explain how
legend-building biographers, hostile historians, and didactic novelists have similarly misrepresented Brown, with virtually all of
them taking sides as to whether he was right or wrong, hero or
horse thief, saint or madman. "Carl Sandburg's Lincoln" relates
how the famous poet enshrined Lincoln as America's greatest
mythical hero, compares that Lincoln to the real-life man, and
ruminates on the persistent confusion of myth with history in this
country. "Ghost Riders in the Sky," pursuing the misuses of history and myth in a concomitant setting, discusses how modern
political advocates exploit the frontier of Lincoln's time to vindicate themselves and flay their opponents.

I do not claim, of course, that *Our Fiery Trial* enjoys the unity
of a narrative or a monograph. But because of their special inter-
relation of subject, theme, and focus, the studies gathered here
do cohere in subtle ways and on several levels. In addition, they
are held together by a unifying argument: the need for unflinching
realism and a humanistic approach in the study of the past. For if
we are ever to appreciate the people of history and learn from their
triumphs and follies, we must avoid the extremes of hagiography
and vilification and try to understand them fairly in the context
of their times. What we need, to quote Martin Duberman, is "less
dogma, more research, and a chastening sense of wonder at the
complexities of human nature." *

And so it was in this spirit that I prepared *Our Fiery Trial*. Three
essays—"God's Stone in the Pool of Slavery," "The Long Shadow
of Lincoln," and "Themes and Variations of a Civil War Trilogy"
—appear here for the first time. "Lincoln's Journey to Emancipation" and "Carl Sandburg's Lincoln" grew out of presentations
given before professional audiences at Amherst, Massachusetts,
and Galesburg, Illinois. The other studies, previously published
in various journals, have all been revised for this book.

* Duberman, *The Uncompleted Past* (New York, 1969), 14.

ONE

STYRON'S WAR AGAINST THE BLACKS

I

ONE of the most disturbing literary storms of our time was that whipped up by William Styron's *Confessions of Nat Turner* (1967), a novel about that prodigious black figure who led the bloody Virginia slave rebellion of 1831. In an "Author's Note," Styron insisted that he had "rarely departed from the *known* facts about Nat Turner" and advertised his book as less a historical novel than "a meditation on history." Then he went on to depict Turner as a sexually crippled bachelor given to masturbation fantasies about white women. Since the real-life Nat Turner had a wife, black scholars and activists alike cried out in protest. Of course they said the novel violated the historical record. Of course they said it perpetuated the white racist stereotype that all black men are obsessed with white women. Of course they damned Styron for emasculating one of their heroes. Of course they fretted that Styron's grandiose claims —a meditation on history indeed!—would invite both blacks and whites to accept the novel as historically accurate.

But few whites listened. On the contrary, most white reviewers heralded Styron's portrait of Nat as a masterpiece. Eminent white historians like C. Vann Woodward testified to its historical brilliance and integrity. When the book became a runaway best-seller and won the Pulitzer Prize, several black authors had taken all they could stand: they collected their own opinions in a volume called *William Styron's Nat Turner: Ten Black Writers Respond* (1968), edited by John Henrik Clarke. "History's potency is mighty," Clarke thundered, quoting Marxist historian Herbert Aptheker. "The oppressed need it for identity and inspiration; oppressors for justification and legitimacy." One needed only to read that to know what would follow. Although the essays by Vincent Harding and Mike Thelwell subjected Styron's novel to valid and incisive criticism, many of the other reviews were party-line diatribes which castigated Styron as an "unreconstructed Southern rebel" and enshrined Nat himself as "a virile, commanding, courageous figure," a military genius and inflexible white-hater whom today's blacks must emulate. Even Harding became polemical, crying out that Styron "has taken my Nat and gone." Styron's sexual portrait ("is it maudlin ineptitude or sheer mockery?") convinced Harding that only Negroes, "out of the bittersweet bowels of our blackness," could interpret their history and their agony.

Predictably, most white reviewers were as hostile to *Ten Black Writers Respond* as the blacks were to Styron's novel. White historians like Eugene Genovese and Martin Duberman argued that Styron did no violence to the general history of slavery, reproved the blacks for their "obscene" and "ruthless" attack on Styron himself, listed all their historical inaccuracies, and punched away at them for inventing their own myths and racial stereotypes. Genovese, for his part, even defended Styron's dismissal of Nat's "alleged" wife and insisted that Styron's doubt-ridden, white-influenced, sexually disturbed bachelor was "a believable Nat Turner." *

With that, black and white historians went to war over Styron in the journals. Letters to the editor and replies to the letters smoked and blazed in *The New York Review of Books*. Rival war camps sprang up on the literary battlefield—one largely white and pro-Styron, the other largely black and anti-Styron. At historical conventions and on the college lecture circuit, Styron tried desperately to defend his novel and vindicate himself, with furious young blacks yelling at him from the floor. Appalling confrontations these were, exposing the racial antagonisms that had long smoldered in the hallowed towers of the intellectual world.

* Contrary to what Genovese and Styron both have said, there is irrefutable contemporary evidence that Nat's wife not only existed but kept his secret papers during the rebellion. See Oates, *The Fires of Jubilee: Nat Turner's Fierce Rebellion* (New York, 1975), *passim*.

And though the fighting has subsided some, the war over Styron's Turner rages on. Today one who embarks on a study of Nat Turner must face a hail of questions from the rival barricades. All right, where do you stand? Are you for Styron or the blacks? And if one refuses to take sides—as I do—then one is fair game for sharpshooters in both camps. Still, I'll take my chances, because I think the war over Styron's Turner carries profound implications about the misuses of history that deserve nonpartisan discussion. And when one clears away all the polemical smoke and debris, one has little choice—if one is faithful to the truth of history— but to damn both their houses.

II

Let me begin with Styron. While he is no racist storyteller (his vignette of the free Negro Isham should disabuse anybody of thinking that he is), Styron was woefully misguided in his presentation of Nat Turner himself. Instead of creating a make-believe slave rebel with an imaginary name, Styron took a real-life human being, used his name and actual historical context, and invented a condition and temperament for him that in major respects contradict the historical record. As a consequence, Styron's novel is an entirely unacceptable account of Nat Turner, as I briefly stated in "Children of Darkness: Nat Turner's Fierce Rebellion," *American Heritage* (October 1973). Because white historians have provided the bulk of Styron's defense, my comment seemed like traitorous sniping from his own ranks. Therefore in a letter to *American Heritage* (February 1974), Styron protested my remarks on two grounds. First, no matter how many fascinating "facts" I had turned up about the rebellion, Turner himself and "his deeper motivations," like those of other "obscure" historical figures, remain conjectural. That is why novels are written about them that should not even strive for complete "accuracy," even if that were possible.

Second, who the hell was I to criticize William Styron? After all, he had "never heard of Professor Oates," so where did Oates get off calling his novel unacceptable? And anyway, other historians "vastly more eminent than Professor Oates" and "certainly more sophisticated" in grasping the difference between history and fiction—he cited Woodward, Genovese, and Duberman—had testified to the historical soundness of his vision of Nat. So Styron felt secure in swatting off my little pot shots and assuring readers of *American Heritage* that his rendition of Nat Turner was correct.

With due respect to the pecking order in the historical profession, I must dispute Styron's argument. For one thing, those historians who defend his vision of Nat Turner may be vastly more eminent than I, but that in itself does not make them or William Styron right. While his novel contains brilliant descriptions of the world of the Old South (its sights, sounds, smells, its contradictions and racial agonies), Styron nevertheless violated the truth —fictional as well as historical—in his portrayal of Nat. The fact is that Nat Turner had a wife and two or possibly more children, so that Styron's depiction of him as a celibate bachelor given to masturbating about creamy-thighed white women is a clear distortion of the truth and an insult to the Nat Turner who really lived. That, in my judgment, is what renders Styron's treatment of Nat Turner imaginatively unacceptable.

Had Styron done his homework thoroughly, which historical novelists are honor-bound to do, he might have documented the "fascinating fact" of Nat's wife and perhaps saved himself from much of the flak that his "vision" of Nat has brought his way. He might have produced a fictional portrait close to the truth of Nat's life, instead of merely dramatizing fanciful psychological theories—*a la* Stanley Elkins—as is the case with *The Confessions*. Styron might also have discovered something about such real-life people as Nathaniel and Lavinia Francis, whom he persistently distorted in his book. Nathaniel, for his part, could not have been "a mean son-of-a-bitch" and "a nigger breaker," as Styron described him, because six free blacks voluntarily resided on his farm. And Lavinia was not "a slab-faced brute" with "a huge goiter." The historical Lavinia was young, slender, and rather pretty, with high cheekbones and a wide and gentle mouth.

My point is that an historical novelist, while free to speculate on deeper motivations, does not have the license to impose on real human beings temperaments and physical traits they did not have, living conditions they did not experience.

And so we come to one of the fundamental lessons in Styron's war against the blacks: the urgent need for historical authenticity and realism in writing about controversial figures of the past, especially those involved in the combustible race issue. Because Styron's portrait of Nat is not authentic, because it is in fact a disturbing misrepresentation of that real-life black man, I protest against the novel. And I am dismayed at the way in which white historians have defended Styron's misrepresentation. After all, it seems only fair to ask how they would react if the controversy were the other way around. Suppose a black author, arguing that Thomas Jefferson's inner life remains a matter of speculation, wrote a novel that depicted him as a secret homosexual, tormented with fellatio fantasies about the virile black men who tilled his fields. Suppose then that black critics, trumpeting the novel as a masterwork, awarded it something like a W. E. B. Du Bois prize for black literature. Dare we imagine how white critics and eminent white historians would respond to that?

III

If one is concerned with authentic history, with history as a source of insight and enlightenment, then one must also grimace at some of the arguments advanced by politicized blacks in the Styron-Turner controversy. Let's start with their attitudes about black history. Because Styron denigrated Nat Turner's manhood, his novel helped convince a good many black intellectuals that white people were incapable of writing honestly, with sensitivity and compassion, about the black past. So in recent years a furious war cry has reverberated through the ranks of certain black authors and critics: that only blacks can tell the real truth about Nat Turner and other black heroes, that only blacks (as Vincent Harding declared) can interpret and write legitimately about the whole black experience because only they have lived that experience and only they can understand it.

For me, that argument is as tyrannical and indefensible as the Southern white supremacists' assertion that only they can understand the South. Or the extreme feminist position that only women can write about women. If this sort of logic were carried through the human race, then only Jews could write about Jews, Indians about Indians, police about police, rapists about rapists, and Alabama governors about Alabama governors. And Styron about Styron. Which of course is absurd. For generations our best literature has demonstrated that through the limitless capacity of imagination, through the ability of human beings to transcend themselves and empathize and suffer with other human beings, artists can create authentic characters—and compose perceptive biographies of historical figures—who may be the opposite of the author's own sex, race, or creed. For example, in *Another Country* (1962), James Baldwin wrote astutely about blacks and whites, men and women, heterosexuals and homosexuals. Moreover, just because Styron maligned the historical Nat Turner does not mean that all white men are blind and insensitive to the black experience. As evidence, I cite André Schwarz-Bart's *A Woman Named Solitude* (1973), a historical novel that combines the author's own compassionate insights with an accurate and extensive knowledge of New World slavery and African history and mythology. The author is a white Jew born in France. Yet his principal characters are two black women who lived and died in slavery in the French West Indies. Schwarz-Bart not only recounts their life stories in authentic historical context but captures their suffering and dignity with a haunting eloquence one cannot forget. *A Woman Named Solitude* stands as a powerful refutation of the argument that a white male writer cannot fathom the black soul, cannot comprehend the black experience.

And now for the matter of history as propaganda. For the purposes of racial protest, many militant blacks have canonized Nat Turner as a white-killing black superman, and have made his name a rallying cry for the present-day black liberation movement, much as white radicals like Truman Nelson have done with John Brown. Why deify Nat? Because, say black activists and politicized intellectuals, only by inflating him into a glorious black god can black brothers and sisters—especially the children —come to identify with him and break the chains of their own oppression. Unless Nat Turner is presented as a powerful and uncompromising he-man (incapable of fear, of doubts, of love for the "honky"), somehow the kids will grow into obsequious Uncle Toms.

Yet is this not political nonsense? As much a travesty on the truth of history as the very novel the blacks despise? Generations of bored white history students testify to the fact that people don't identify with flawless saints and romanticized immortals. They identify with real-life historical figures who suffered, struggled, triumphed sometimes and failed sometimes, just like people in our time. Therefore won't black children the more readily appreciate Nat Turner if they are told the full dimensions of his struggle? That he did indeed break his chains and rise up in insurrection and direct the murder of white Southerners because slavery had maimed and murdered Negroes? But that he also felt affection for his first master, Old Benjamin Turner, who approved of Nat's literacy and encouraged him to read the Bible? And that Nat had affection for his last master and mistress as well—Joseph and Sally Travis—who were the first to perish in his war for slave liberation? As Harold Cruse has observed, slavery locked blacks and whites together in a purgatory of love and hate. And Nat suffered in that purgatory, smoldering with resentment at his enslavement and that of his people, enjoying just enough freedom as a slave preacher to want complete freedom, until at last he felt himself called by God to revolt. Yet Nat dreaded to commence because of the violence that would attend rebellion. He wavered, almost gave it up, until a heavenly sign convinced him that his God—the vengeful Jehovah of the Old Testament—wanted him to rise up in spite of his misgivings. Yet in the course of the revolt he displayed a fatal irresolution about slaughtering white people himself—which was entirely human for a man of his supreme intelligence and sensitivity. After the rebellion was over and he came to trial in Jerusalem, Virginia, he was fiercely unrepentant and confronted his white captors with a pride and defiance that awed them. Yet before the revolt, this same Nat Turner baptized and ministered to a sick, demoralized white man because Preacher Nat felt compassion for him.

Nat Turner was a complex and paradoxical man, a victim of a violent system who in the end struck back with retributive violence. At the age of thirty-one, he was hanged in Virginia, one of the final casualties in an insurrection and an ensuing white reign of terror that demonstrated with blazing clarity what Frederick Douglass said of slavery—that it brutalized everybody, black and white alike. The historical Turner, with all his strength and human frailty, his loves and hatreds, his family cares and messianic posturings, his liberating visions and bloody doom, lived a life that affords profound insight into the tragic consequences of man's inhumanity to his fellow man. But we will never know this if Nat is removed from the reality of his own time and made a slogan and a shibboleth for modern activists—or if he is used as a mouthpiece for the fantasies and unfounded suppositions of a modern novelist.

TWO

GOD'S STONE IN THE POOL OF SLAVERY

I

On a rainswept October night in 1859, grizzled old John Brown led a handful of revolutionaries —most of them young, five of them black—in a surprise attack against Harpers Ferry in northern Virginia, in what Brown envisioned as the first blow in an all-out war for slave liberation. With his twenty-one followers, he intended to incite a Southern-wide slave revolt and to establish a black state in the Southern mountains. Or, failing that, he hoped to ignite a sectional holocaust between North and South in which slavery would be destroyed.

For fifty-nine-year-old John Brown, a failure in virtually everything he had ever tried, this was the supreme moment of his life, the moment he had been working for since he had committed himself to violence in the Kansas civil war of 1856. All the years of trial, of affliction and sorrow, were behind him now. He and his men were going to liberate some four million human beings from bondage, thereby removing a monstrous wrong from American society. For Brown, slavery was an egregious "sin against God," a sin that violated the commandments of an all-wise, all-powerful Providence, and that contradicted the Declaration of Independence, too, which guaranteed all men the right to life, liberty, and the pursuit of happiness. Yes, slavery was *"foul and loathsome,"* Brown believed, a *"rotten whore"* of an institution which was not only criminally unjust to Negroes, but which offended him personally. When he was twelve years old, he had

watched with growing rage—a rage he could not then articulate—
as a Michigan innkeeper beat a slave boy with an iron fire shovel.
In addition to his intense religious convictions, slavery violated
Brown's secular views as well: his passionate commitment to the
nuclear family (he had read about the inhuman breakup of slave
families), his belief in the right of all men to enjoy the fruits of
their labor and to raise themselves above the condition of their
birth. Yet, instead of eradicating slavery, the United States had
institutionalized that cruel institution, surrounding it with a net-
work of legal and political safeguards quite as though the Declaration of Independence did not exist. Such hypocrisy enraged Brown.
How could Americans sanction slavery and yet proclaim theirs
the freest and most enlightened nation in the world? By 1859 he
thought it impossible to remove slavery through regular political
channels. For Southerners and their Northern allies dominated the
crucial branches of the federal government and were using these
agencies not only to preserve and perpetuate slavery, but also to
extend it into the Western territories as well. Moreover, the United
States Supreme Court, controlled by Southern Democrats, had
denied Negroes the right of United States citizenship and had for-
bidden Congress to exclude slavery from the public lands. And in
Brown's opinion few Northerners seemed to care. Northern Democrats, he declared, were all "doughfaces" who enjoyed licking up
"Southern spittle." Republicans were too "wishy-washy" about
slavery to do anything about that institution. And the bona fide
abolitionists were "milk-and-water" pacifists who preferred talk
to action. By the late 1850s, Brown asserted, slavery had become
too entrenched in American life ever to be expunged except by
revolutionary violence—and by the extermination of this entire
generation of men, women, and children, if that were the will of
Almighty God. Such statements had electrified New England hu-
manitarians like Ralph Waldo Emerson—who thought Brown was
speaking symbolically—and had won him the outright support
of six influential Northern reformers, who organized a secret
committee to raise guns and money for his projected Virginia
invasion.

On the eve of the attack, one or two of Brown's backers began
to doubt the wisdom of the operation, but the old man was un-
daunted. He was convinced that Northern free blacks and Southern slaves would rally to his standard. He was equally certain that

he was an instrument in the hands of God, a special angel of death called to remove slavery with the sword. So deeply did Brown—a devout Calvinist all his life—believe that God was directing the Harpers Ferry enterprise, that he thought it unnecessary to make battle plans, to examine the mountainous terrain about Harpers Ferry, to send out agents to contact slaves in the neighborhood, to work out escape plans in case militia or federal troops should mobilize. God would hurl Brown like a stone "into the black pool of slavery" and God alone would determine the outcome.

The outcome was never much in doubt. Brown and his little army seized the federal arsenal at Harpers Ferry and threw the town into bedlam. But militiamen soon surrounded the arsenal, and federal troops under Robert E. Lee, moving up from Washington at a killing pace, stormed the fire-engine house and captured the gnarled old captain and his surviving raiders. Virginia authorities brought Brown to a speedy trial and sentenced him to hang for murder, for inciting slaves to insurrection, and for treason against Virginia (although he was not a citizen of that state). But before he went to the gallows, Brown uttered some of the most eloquent words ever to come from a condemned man. What he said was not always the truth—he denied, for example, that he had ever intended to provoke a slave rebellion—but he did not care about that now. What he cared about was enlisting widespread Northern support for Negro freedom by playing on his own courage and self-sacrifice—and by playing on white guilts. "If it is deemed necessary," he told the Virginia court (and a divided nation beyond), "that I should forfeit my life for the furtherance of the ends of justice and mingle my blood with the blood of millions in this slave country whose rights are disregarded by wicked, cruel, and unjust enactments, I say let it be done."

Brown's majestic statements, and the moral complexities surrounding the Harpers Ferry attack, plunged the North into what seemed a confusion of voices. The abolitionists, constituting a small minority there, heralded Brown as a saint who made the gallows—as Emerson phrased it—as glorious as the cross. This did not mean that the abolitionists now embraced revolutionary violence to rid the country of slavery. On the contrary, most of them remained committed to nonviolent protest. But in Brown they had an engaging symbol—of noble idealism and Christian sacrifice—and they used that symbol in a renewed effort to make

Americans face the slavery curse forthrightly. Other Northerners agreed that Harpers Ferry involved extenuating circumstances— Brown's opposition to slavery was admirable—but thought the raid itself a criminal act which should not go unpunished. On the other hand, most members of the Republican party, with an eye on forthcoming state elections, disparaged Brown as a solitary fanatic who deserved to be hanged. And what they said reflected the opinions of a majority of Northern whites, who not only condemned Brown for taking the law into his own hands, but asserted the right of Southerners to own Negro slaves.

Southerners, though, were fatefully unable to believe that the mass of conservative Northern opinion was typical of the region. So Southern Democrats and their Northern colleagues branded the raid as a Republican party conspiracy, a wild and vicious scheme to destroy the whole Southern "way of life." While the Republicans emphatically denied the charge, few in the South listened. The Virginia General Assembly, in an outburst of fear and defiance, declared that not just the "Black" Republicans, but the entire North was behind Harpers Ferry: the work of "fanatics" —all Northerners were fanatics—who wanted to incite the slaves to rape and murder. Even though no slaves had risen to join Brown, rumors of slave "stampedes" and abolitionist invasions swept across the South, plunging the region into convulsions of hysteria. In a miasma of imagined revolts and attacks, Southerners mobilized their militia and slave patrols, imprisoned unattended slaves and suspicious-looking strangers, and imposed severe discipline in the slave compounds. As one historian phrased it, "The raid of twenty-two men on one Virginia town had sent a spasm of uneasiness, resentment, and precautionary zeal from the Potomac to the Gulf."

In truth, the raid had done a good deal more than that: it had so alarmed Southern whites that henceforth any compromise between them and Northern Republicans was impossible. And nobody was more exultant about the effects of Harpers Ferry than Southern secessionists, who used Brown's name to whip Southern crowds into a frenzy of anti-Republican, anti-Northern hatred. Harpers Ferry, raged one secessionist, "is the first act in the grand tragedy of emancipation, and the subjugation of the South in bloody treason.... The vanguard of the great army intended for our subjugation has crossed our borders on Southern soil and shed

Southern blood." The only solution for the South, the only way to save "our wives and daughters," was secession and an independent, slaveholding confederacy.

II

Such massive overreaction to Brown's abortive venture may seem difficult to comprehend. After all, nothing really had happened. No slave rebellion had occurred, Brown had been summarily hanged, most Northerners thought he deserved it. But Southerners of that time were in no mood to treat Harpers Ferry as an isolated incident. For them, Brown's attack carried sinister implications about the entire past and future of the American Union; and it played on deep-seated anxieties about slavery—and about the safety of the South in the Union—that had been growing for decades.

In fact, from the very beginning of the nation, the planters—the South's master class—had felt uneasy about their slave regime. At the federal convention of 1787, Southern slaveowners refused to discuss the slavery issue, compelling the other delegates to avoid it or to forget about creating a stronger Union. So, apart from allowing the federal Congress to abolish the foreign slave trade (which it subsequently did), the Constitution maintained "a conspiracy of silence" about the slavery problem. In the 1790s, Southern congressmen demanded that all antislavery petitions be tabled, insisting that such documents were "an entering wedge for total emancipation." Although Thomas Jefferson and other enlightened Southerners talked about abolishing slavery in the South, few of them put their words into action. Their racist constituents would never have accepted emancipation anyway, even if it were gradual and even if slaveowners were compensated for their loss.

Why was this so? Because slavery in the South was always more than a labor device; it was also a rigid system of racial control to maintain white supremacy in a region brimming with Negroes. In this respect, slavery was quite as important to the mass of non-slaveholding whites—always a majority in the Old South—as to the small planter elite that controlled the region. For no matter how low the poor whites sank, no matter how miserable their lives, they were still better than the "nigger" in the levees and cotton fields. They were still white men. Moreover, yeomen and poor whites alike aspired to own Negroes, because slave owner-ship in the Old South was a tremendous status symbol. Many of these whites were also "expectant" planters who hoped some day to make a lot of money and live in a big white house like the gentry they admired and envied. Such aspirations and feelings melted away whatever class antagonism might have existed in the Old South and united nearly all whites against the Negro him-self—"our internal foe," Virginians called him, a common enemy in their midst, a sinister being of an alien and "inferior" race who if liberated would bring about social chaos and racial catastrophe.*

By the 1820s, the Old South seemed on the verge of another kind of catastrophe. A series of insurrection panics rocked the Deep South, especially the South Carolina tidewater where blacks heavily outnumbered whites. In 1822, authorities in Charles-ton uncovered a shocking slave plot—that of Denmark Vesey—which called for an all-out race war against the whites. Next there occurred the Charleston fire scare and the Georgetown conspiracy. While neither of these ranked as a rebellion, South Carolinians were terror-stricken. Then came 1831 and the bloody Nat Turner revolt in southeastern Virginia. A slave preacher who believed himself an instrument of God, Turner led sixty or seventy slave insurgents on a gruesome rampage: they hacked some sixty whites to death, including women and children. At last the militia crushed the rebellion and executed Turner and twenty other blacks, but not before vengeful whites had slaughtered more than 120 innocent Negroes.

The Turner uprising shook the Old South to its foundations. For who could be safe now in so grim and treacherous a time? How many more revolts would follow? Who among one's own slaves could be trusted? Virginians were so alarmed that they considered liberating all their slaves and then colonizing them at state ex-pense. But in a dramatic debate over the feasibility of manumis-

---

* Paradoxically, of course, Southern slaveowners often felt genuine affection for their Negroes (as long as they kept in their places), taught them Christianity, and pampered their house servants until some felt superior to "po white trash." And all the while Southerners trumpeted the glories of racial purity, many white slaveowners copulated clandestinely with black women.

sion, the Virginia legislature concluded that colonization was too costly and too complicated to implement. And since they were not about to emancipate the blacks and leave them as free people in their state, Virginians rejected abolition outright. Then they set about revising their slave codes and restricting their blacks so severely that they could never again mount an insurrection. Even so, whites in Virginia and everywhere else in the South could never escape the fear that somewhere, maybe in their own slave quarters, another Nat Turner was plotting to rise up and slit their throats.

For intimidated Southerners, it was no mere coincidence that the Turner rebellion came at a time of rising abolitionist militancy in the North. In fact, just six months before the Turner uprising, William Lloyd Garrison began publishing the *Liberator* in Boston, demanding in bold, strident editorials that the slaves be immediately and unconditionally emancipated. Desperately needing somebody to blame for Turner besides themselves, Southerners insisted that Garrison's rhetoric had incited the Turner outbreak, insisted that all abolitionists were bloodthirsty fanatics who wanted to obliterate the South in a carnage of racial violence. While this was hardly true (Garrison and his followers were Christian pacifists), Southerners believed what they wanted to believe. From 1831 on, slave rebellion and Yankee abolitionism were synonymous in the Southern mind.

Nor were threats to the South confined to the United States. A powerful antislavery movement seemed to be sweeping the entire Western world. In the 1830s, Great Britain abolished slavery in the Empire, and impassioned English emancipators came to crusade in America as well. Inevitably, Southerners came to view their region as a lonely slave outpost in a hostile, changing world. Unable to change themselves, unable to free their blacks and surrender their cherished way of life, Southerners embarked on the Great Southern Reaction of the 1830s and 1840s, during which the Old South, threatened it seemed by internal and external enemies, became a closed, martial society determined to defend its slave-based civilization at all costs. Southern postmasters set about confiscating all abolitionist literature, lest these "incendiary" tracts invite the slaves to violence. Southerners also tightened up slave discipline, refusing to let blacks visit other plantations and vowing to hang any Negro who even looked rebellious. At the same time, Southerners eliminated slave schools and churches, revived their old slave patrols, and strengthened their militia forces. By the 1840s the Old South had devised such an oppressive slave system that organized insurrection was next to impossible.

Freedom of thought in the South was also difficult, as Southern zealots stamped out dissent at home and demanded total conformity to the Southern way. They seized "anti-Southern" books and burned them, expelled from classrooms any teacher suspected of abolitionist tendencies, and branded as a traitor anybody who questioned the right of slavery. Some states actually passed sedition laws and other restrictive measures which prohibited Negroes and whites alike from criticizing the peculiar institution.

In reaction to the abolitionists, Southern spokesmen began proclaiming the institution a positive good, asserting that it was justified by history, condoned by the Bible, and ordained by God from the beginning of time. They argued that "niggers" were subhuman anyway and belonged in chains as naturally as cattle in pens. Such inferior brutes were not fit for liberty and equality; these were rights reserved only for white men (for Anglo-Saxon white men). In fact, Southerners were doing "niggers" a huge Christian favor by enslaving them. On the floor of the United States Senate, John C. Calhoun declared slavery "a good—a positive good" and warned that it was indispensable for race control and could not be abolished "without drenching the country in blood." And cranky George Fitzhugh, writing pro-Southern tracts in a ramshackle, bat-ridden Virginia plantation, extolled Southern planters as enlightened reactionaries who ruled an insulated slave community, family based and proudly provincial. But to attain complete security, Fitzhugh contended, Southerners must free themselves from the competitive, market economy which governed the modern world; they must destroy capitalism—or "free society"—and revive the halcyon days of precapitalist Europe. Then the master class should enslave all workers, white as well as black, and the world would enjoy supreme order and stability. While few planters embraced Fitzhugh's economic views, they emphatically shared his assessment of the abolitionists. "For thirty years," Fitzhugh growled, "the South has been a field on which abolitionists, foreign and domestic, have carried on offensive warfare. Let us now, in turn, act on the offensive, transfer the seat of war, and invade the enemy's territory."

III

Southern leaders were anxious indeed to take the offensive, because only by doing so, they believed, could the South survive in a hostile world. They strove harder than ever to control the federal government, in order to prevent Northerners from enacting an abolition law or adopting any other measure that might harm the South. Because Southerners dominated the Democrats, the nation's majority party, they generally controlled the presidency, the Cabinet, the Senate, and the Supreme Court from the 1840s to 1860. They became consummate obstructionists, demolishing any bill that might facilitate the growth of the free states or the Yankee business community. In their zeal, Southerners seemed oblivious to the fact that Northern big businessmen were not their enemies but their friends; most of these businessmen despised the abolitionists and went out of their way to appease the South, because Southerners bought their manufactured goods and sold them cotton. Northern capitalists would go to almost any length to hold the Union together with slavery, because they believed disunion would be economically devastating.

Until 1859, most Southerners wanted to remain in the Union, but at a high price. In addition to manipulating the federal government, they sought to open the Western territories to unrestrained slavery expansion. In fact, proslavery Missourians and other Southerners vowed to seize the new territory of Kansas and make it a gateway for slave expansion to the Pacific, thus creating a greater South with a world outlet on two oceans. In the late 1850s, Southern leaders in Washington clamored for a federal law guaranteeing what they regarded as their constitutional right to take slaves into the territories. In part, this was to prevent the free states from invading the West and ringing the South with hostile satellite territories. It would also set a precedent so that slavery could expand into Cuba and Central America, should the United States acquire those lands as Southern expansionists advocated.

In their efforts to extend slavery, Southern Democrats collided dramatically with the newly formed Republican party, a coalition of Northern free-soil elements out to contain slavery and dismantle Southern power in Washington. From 1856 on, Southern politicians engaged in a life-or-death struggle with the Republican party, regarding it as a demonic threat to slavery and the whole Southern way of life based on that institution.

The Republicans, for their part, denied any intention of menacing the South. While they were determined to exclude slavery from the territories, they vowed to leave it alone in the Southern states where it already existed. But the Southern people—who for twenty years had lived in a closed and suspicious society, dedicated to suppressing dissent and defending slavery—refused to believe anything the Republicans said. Were they not opposed to slavery in the territories? Then they must be against it in the South as well. Did Republicans not denounce slavery as an evil which must perish some day? Then all Republicans must be abolitionists, radicals, and fanatics. Never mind their disavowals. Never mind their talk about "ultimate" extinction. Extinction was extinction. Once the Republicans attained power, pledges to leave slavery alone in the South would disappear like any other campaign promise, and the next thing Southerners would know, Republican troops would be invading their farms and plantations and liberating the slaves at gun point. "I shudder to contemplate it!" cried an Alabama white man. "What social monstrosities, what desolated fields, what civil broils, what robberies, rapes, and murders of the poorer whites by the emancipated blacks would then disfigure the whole fair face of this prosperous, smiling, and happy Southern land."

Anti-Republican feelings pervaded all classes in the Old South, and the fire-eaters—those already agitating for Southern independence—rushed to capitalize on those sentiments. On the stump and in the press, these spirited demagogues distorted Republican speeches and wrenched remarks out of context, molding these into inflammatory slogans to demonstrate that Republicans were warmongering abolitionists and that Southerners, for their own safety, had to get out of the Union. This is not to say that Southern discontent was a "manufactured crisis," created by a small bunch of rabble-rousers. On the contrary, the fire-eaters were telling Southern crowds precisely what they wanted to hear. Had Abraham Lincoln not proclaimed that a house divided against itself could not stand, that this nation could not endure half slave and half free? Had William H. Seward of New York not declared that North and South were locked in an irrepressible conflict? Were such statements not proof that Republicans desired a sectional war? Although both Seward and Lincoln hotly denied that they desired any such thing, their disclaimers fell on deaf ears.

IV

By 1859, tensions between Republicans and Southern whites were at a combustible state. All that was needed was an overt act against the South—a spark to set a confligration roaring. And that spark came in the form of John Brown, who for two years had been secretly plotting his bold and audacious attack against slavery in Virginia. That attack, one must remember, had alternative objectives: should it fail, Brown had repeatedly argued, it would nevertheless ignite a sectional powder keg that might explode into civil war. Though often maligned as a demented dreamer, Brown in one respect was an extremely perceptive man: he understood the depth of Southern anxieties about slavery, understood that all he had to do—being a Northerner and an abolitionist—was to set foot in the South with a gun, announce that he was here to free the slaves, and the effect on the South would be cataclysmic.

And so the Harpers Ferry raid took place. And so the South reacted with even greater hysteria than had followed Nat Turner's uprising. For thousands of Southerners, from poor whites in South Carolina to rich cotton planters in Mississippi, Harpers Ferry was the inevitable result of the "abolitionist" doctrines of the Republican party; the attack was dramatic, conclusive proof that slave insurrection was what the "Black" Republicans had wanted all along. From Harpers Ferry on, the Republican party and Brown-style revolutionary violence were forged like a ring of steel in the Southern mind.

Harpers Ferry, in sum, ensured that some kind of violent rupture would take place should the Republicans win the presidential election of 1860. There were, of course, a number of loyal Unionists in the South who pleaded for reason and restraint, who beseeched their fellow Southerners to wait for an overt Republican act against them before they did anything rash. For most, though, Brown's raid had been all the overt action they needed. "The Harper's Ferry invasion," exclaimed the Richmond *Enquirer*, "has advanced the cause of Disunion more than any other event that has happened since the formation of the Government." "I have said of Mr. Seward and his followers," cried a state senator of Mississippi, "that they are our enemies and we are theirs. He has declared that there is an 'irrepressible conflict' between us. So there is! He and his followers have declared war upon us, and I am for fighting it out to the bitter end."

And to the bitter end, the Republicans kept trying to reach the South, kept denying any complicity in Brown's attack. "You charge that we stir up insurrections among your slaves," Lincoln told the South in his 1860 address at Cooper Union. "We deny it; and what is your proof? Harper's Ferry! John Brown!! John Brown was no Republican; and you have failed to implicate a single Republican in his Harper's Ferry enterprise." After he was nominated for the presidency and the Southern press viciously assailed him, Lincoln could not fathom why Southerners were so incensed. What had the Republicans done to them? What Southern rights had they violated? Did not Southerners still have the fugitive slave law? Did they not have the same Constitution they had lived under for seventy-odd years? "Why all this excitement?" he asked a crowd at Cleveland, Ohio. "Why all these complaints?" He wrote Alexander H. Stephens of Georgia: "Do the people of the South really entertain fears that a Republican administration would, *directly,* or *indirectly,* interfere with their slaves . . . ? If they do, I wish to assure you, as once a friend, and still, I hope, not an enemy, that there is no cause for such fears." Lincoln added: "I suppose, however, this does not meet the case. You think slavery is *right* and ought to be extended; while we think it is *wrong* and ought to be restricted. That I suppose is the rub. It certainly is the only substantial difference between us."

Stephens and other Southern Unionists begged Lincoln to issue a public statement about his views. But he declined, remarking that he had made his opinions explicitly clear in previous speeches and that Southern militants would misconstrue anything he said. He was undoubtedly right. And anyway, Republicans and Southern whites were no longer speaking the same language. Words like *rights* and *constitution,* like *freedom* and *self-government,* meant one thing to the Republicans and quite another to distraught Southerners. For the latter, freedom meant escape from threats and invasions. And rights meant the right of white supremacy

(Southern style), of self-determination and Southern independence. And Southerners were now ready for independence, if that
was what it took to protect their slave-based social order from the
"Black" Republican menace.

So when Lincoln was elected president, the seven states of the
Deep South—with their heavy concentration of slaves—seceded
from the Union. As the editor of the *Montgomery Mail* explained:
"In the struggle for maintaining the ascendancy of our race in the
South—our home—we see no chance for victory but in withdraw-
ing from the Union. To remain in the Union is to lose all that
white men hold dear in government. We vote to get out."

For the Republicans, all this was hard to comprehend. They had
repeatedly asserted that they had no intention of freeing the slaves
in the Southern states. And in any case, the Democrats, though
divided themselves, had still won control of Congress and could
demolish any abolition bill introduced there. But the Deep South
was intractable all the same. And Lincoln himself decided to
hold firm. He had won the presidency in a fair and legal contest.
He would not compromise his election mandate. He would preserve the Union and the principle of self-government on which
the Union was based: the right of a free people to choose their
leaders and to expect the losers to acquiesce in that decision.
And so the fateful events raced by in rapid-fire sequence: Fort
Sumter, Lincoln's call for troops, the secession of the upper South,
and the beginning of a civil war in which slavery itself would perish—the very thing old John Brown had hoped and prayed would
be the ultimate consequences of the Harpers Ferry raid.

THREE

JOHN BROWN AND HIS JUDGES

I

AMERICANS have always found it difficult to write fairly about controversial figures in their past, and this has been especially true of John Brown. Since he died on the gallows for attacking Harpers Ferry, those who have dealt with him—biographers, poets, novelists, essayists, and, alas, professional historians—have with rare exception been either passionately for or against the man. Either Brown was *right* or he was *wrong*. Either he was an authentic and immortal hero who sacrificed his life so that America's "poor, despised Africans" might be free, or he was a "mean, terrible, vicious man," a demented horse thief, a murderer, a psychopath. For over one hundred years, American writers—popular and scholarly alike—have engaged in such heated controversy over whether Brown was right or wrong, sane or crazy, hero or fanatic, that scarcely anyone has taken the time to try to understand him.

The legend of Brown as hero emerged from a succession of worshipful biographies published between 1860 and 1910. Those written by James Redpath, Franklin B. Sanborn, and Richard J. Hinton —all of whom had been friends and associates of Brown—portrayed him as a deeply principled "Puritan soldier," "an idealist with a human intent," "a simple, brave, heroic person, incapable of anything selfish or base." The legend-builders did not always agree on facts. Redpath, the propagandist of the Brown legend, asserted that the Old Hero did not commit the Pottawatomie murders in Kansas, that he was somewhere else when they occurred. Sanborn, followed by Hinton, gave evidence that Brown had instigated the massacre, but argued that he was justified in doing so, inasmuch as the victims were crude, violent, proslavery "poor whites" who would likely have massacred Brown and his free-state neighbors had he not killed them first. But facts aside, all three biographers, disregarding unfavorable aspects of Brown's character and career, presented him as a great man in the manner of Samson, Hercules, and Oliver Cromwell—a steadfast warrior who saved Kansas for liberty in 1856 and then gave his life in Virginia so that the slaves might be free. He was "a saint," Hinton proclaimed; "Our bravest martyr," said Redpath. Brown was as heroic as Lincoln and as noble as Socrates, declared Sanborn, one of the Secret Six who furnished Brown with guns and money for the Virginia invasion. "What he did in Kansas for a single State, he did in Virginia for the whole nation,—nay, for the whole world."

Other early biographies—those by Richard D. Webb, Hermann von Holst, Joseph Edgar Chamberlin, William E. Connelley, and W. E. Burghart Du Bois, none of whom had been associated with Brown, but all of whom idolized what he stood for—also depicted the Old Hero in legendary terms. Connelley, rebutting those writers and politicians who had attacked the Brown legend in post-Civil War Kansas, argued that the Pottawatomie massacre was "the most important work of John Brown in Kansas" and that he was *still* a martyr, no matter what his detractors said. The Du Bois volume, while exhibiting a cheerful disregard for factual accuracy, was a scathing indictment of slavery and an impassioned defense of Brown as a revolutionary symbol, as a man who was "eternally right" in his decision to destroy an institution that was "eternally wrong."

The early biographies, then, were either defenses or eulogies of Brown as the abolitionist martyr. None of them attempted to examine the whole range of Brown's personality, to account for his mistakes and faults (his egotism, cruelty, intolerance, self-righteousness) as well as his courage and uncompromising abolitionism.

II

The first serious effort to give a rounded portrait of the Old Hero was Oswald Garrison Villard's now classic *John Brown, 1800–1859: A Biography Fifty Years After*, published initially in 1910 and reissued in a second edition, without textual revision, in 1943. Based on prodigious research in manuscript and printed sources and on numerous interviews with Brown's surviving relatives and friends, Villard's book was a compendium of not always well-digested facts, letters, and recollections. Yet such a compendium is useful indeed, not only for the research scholar, but for anyone who might want to know about some of the more controversial aspects of Brown's life. Although Villard was a pacifist and a deeply committed humanitarian who sympathized with Brown, he was not afraid to quote from those who recalled how severe Brown had been with his children and his employees and how stubborn and incompetent he had been as a businessman. Still, Villard tended to apologize for the harsher sides of Brown's personality, and the interpretation of Brown that emerged from his encyclopedic work was a tempered version of the traditional view. True, Villard conceded, Brown had made mistakes in his life. True, he had directed that "bloody crime" on Pottawatomie Creek in Kansas, a crime that his "wealth of self-sacrifice, and the nobility of his aims," could not justify. But, the Pottawatomie massacre aside, Brown was still a hero doing battle with injustice, a man who possessed "straightforward unselfishness" and a willingness "to suffer for others"—traits dramatically exhibited when he made his sacrifice "for the altar of liberty" at Harpers Ferry and on the gallows at Charlestown, Virginia. Thus Villard believed that the "story of John Brown will ever confront the spirit of despotism, when men are struggling to throw off the shackles of social or political or physical slavery. His own country, while admitting his mistakes without undue palliation or excuse, will forever acknowledge the divine that was in him by the side of what was human or faulty, and blind and wrong. It will cherish the memory of the prisoner of Charlestown in 1859 as at once a sacred, a solemn and an inspiring American heritage."

While Villard deserves credit for the extensiveness of his research and for his sincere effort to be fair and honest in recounting Brown's life, his biography left several vital questions unanswered. For one thing, Villard only paid lip service to Brown's "Puritan" religion; he made no attempt to show how Brown's religious beliefs, based in large measure on the mystical New Light Calvinism of Jonathan Edwards, not only shaped his vision of himself in the world and his nonconformist brand of abolitionism, but also influenced his Harpers Ferry plans. Theologically, Brown was an orthodox nineteenth-century Calvinist who believed in fore-ordination, the doctrine of election, innate depravity, and in man's total dependence on a just and omnipotent God. He believed, too, that once God saved "poor dependent, sinning, & self condemned mortals" like himself, then God remained a constant, all-powerful, directive force in his life. Brown's notion that God had chosen him to free the slaves—a notion that lay behind his invasion of Virginia—was an outgrowth of his intense Calvinist faith.

If Villard did not adequately deal with Brown's religion, he also failed to show how Brown was influenced by his environment. For example, what effect did the abolitionist movement in Ohio—and in the North at large—have in shaping Brown's own anti-slavery views? How much did his work on the Underground Railroad, and his association with such Negro leaders as Frederick Douglass and Henry Highland Garnet, contribute to his growing conviction that slavery could only be destroyed by violence? And when exactly did Brown's decision to fight slavery in the South become the "greatest or principal object" of his life?

Villard did address himself to the latter question, but his answer is open to dispute. He asserted that Brown was committed to the destruction of slavery from about 1846 on—in other words, all other considerations were of secondary importance—and that by 1855 he had more or less perfected a plan that called for full-scale guerrilla warfare against slavery in the South. He might have put that plan into operation around 1856 had not trouble broken out in Kansas, compelling him to fight slavery there before he undertook the grand scheme. In support of his thesis, Villard relied chiefly on recollections of Brown's children and acquaintances, given long after the Civil War, and on memorandum entries in the second volume of Brown's private notebooks. Among other things, these entries contained references to Mina's guerrilla operations in Spain during the Napoleonic Wars and included a list of American cities and towns, most of them in the South, where federal forts or arsenals were located. Villard claimed that these notes were "probably recorded early in 1855" and consequently supported the contention of some members of the Brown family that Brown planned an invasion of the South, to commence at Harpers Ferry, before he went to Kansas.

In point of fact, the entries in question were made not in 1855, but in the summer of 1857—*after* Brown's experiences in the Kansas civil war. The evidence seems fairly convincing that Brown did not conceive the Harpers Ferry or Virginia scheme, which involved a slave insurrection in the South, until the fall of 1856 or spring of 1857, as a result of his own private war against the "Slave Power" which began with the Pottawatomie massacre.

Not that Brown lacked ideas about opposing the South with force before that time. On the contrary, he appears to have developed by 1847 a secret project called the Subterranean Pass Way, which probably derived from his experiences with the Ohio Underground Railroad. The project called for an armed guerrilla contingent, with Brown as commander, to run slaves out of the South through the Allegheny Mountains (long an escape route for fugitives). In Brown's mind, these operations would reduce the value of slave property, thereby rendering the institution so "insecure" that Southerners would have to abolish it themselves. Frederick Douglass, who claimed that Brown revealed this plan to him in 1847 (and there seems no reason to dispute him), said that Brown did not intend to incite an insurrection at this time. But he was quite prepared to fight slaveowners in the mountains, because he did not believe they could "be induced to give up their slaves, until they felt a big stick about their heads." The Subterranean Pass Way scheme was a sort of hobby of Brown's from 1847 until he left for Kansas in 1855. While the scheme never got beyond the planning stage, it clearly became the basis of his Harpers Ferry project.

Villard's assertion that Brown went to Kansas in 1855 to fight for freedom, without giving a thought to settlement there, is inaccurate. The evidence indicates that Brown initially planned to follow his sons to the Territory to engage in surveying and investigate business prospects there. By relocating in Kansas and later bringing out his family from their farm in upstate New York, he could do his part to settle the Territory with antislavery pioneers who would vote to make it free. But when John Jr. wrote that business opportunities were not promising in Kansas, when he described how a great war between freedom and slavery was about to begin there, beseeching his father to gather a number of guns for free-state forces, Brown altered his original intentions for going to Kansas. He solicited weapons in New York, Massachusetts, and Ohio, and set out for the Territory to fight the armies of the "Slave Power," should war break out there as John Jr. had predicted.

Villard's assessment of Brown's role in the Kansas troubles of 1855 and 1856 contained some errors and overstatements, but Villard was not so "blind" in his "hero-worship" of Brown as James C. Malin charged. In all fairness to Villard, he dismissed as myth the contention that Brown saved Kansas for freedom. He pointed out that "no one man decided the fate of Kansas" and that much of Brown's lone-hand activities in the summer of 1856 actually impeded the free-state cause.

Villard stated that once peace had been restored to Kansas, Brown turned back to his Virginia plan, which he had set aside in 1855, and traveled east to solicit guns and money for that operation as well as for any additional fighting he might have to undertake in the Territory. While Villard provided a mass of information about Brown's movements from 1857 to 1859—as he gathered supporters and recruits for his Virginia scheme—Brown the complex and messianic revolutionary figure never came alive in Villard's pages. The man was lost in a vortex of facts and block quotations. Nor did Villard offer any real insights into the personalities and motivations of the six abolitionist reformers who supported Brown—Franklin B. Sanborn. Thomas Wentworth Higginson, Gerrit Smith, Theodore Parker, George Luther Stearns, and Samuel Gridley Howe. The closest Villard came to explaining Brown's own motives (beyond an implacable opposition to slavery) was the following declaration: "Something compelled him to attack slavery by force of arms, and to that impulse he yielded." Given little more than that, one sets the book aside knowing a great deal of factual information, but with only scant understanding of Brown himself, of what it was that convinced him and his secret backers that only violence could solve the slavery problem of their time.

III

Because Villard portrayed Brown as the immortal if imperfect hero (one capable of errors), he was criticized both by Brown's defenders and his detractors.* The most scathing denunciation came from Hill Peebles Wilson, a Kansas politician who claimed that he had been an admirer of Brown until he learned "the facts." Then he discovered that the Old Hero was not a hero at all, but a crook. After Villard published his "jargon of facts and fancies," his "fulsome panegyrics" and "extravagantly illogical attributes" about Brown, Wilson decided to tell the public "the truth." The result was his *John Brown, Soldier of Fortune: A Critique*, which was privately printed in Lawrence, Kansas, in 1913. Drawing those facts from Villard that would suit his thesis, Wilson categorized Brown as a swindler even before he went to Kansas, citing as evidence his "fraudulent and criminal" business ventures, especially in Ohio (an accusation that itself was a gross distortion of the record). Wilson asserted that Brown migrated to Kansas in hopes that some criminal opportunity would turn up, that he murdered those five men on Pottawatomie Creek to steal their horses and prevent them from testifying against him in the pro-slavery court, that he looted and plundered under the pretext of fighting for the free-state cause, and that ultimately he sought to pursue his nefarious activities on a larger scale by invading the South. If Brown had a tradition, said Wilson, it was not as a great hero, but as "a soldier of fortune, an adventurer. He will take his place in history as such; and will rank among adventurers as Napoleon ranks among marshals; as Captain Kidd among pirates; and as Jonathan Wild among thieves."

Wilson's book is so biased and so rife with unsupported conjecture that nobody should take it seriously as history. Indeed, it is not history at all but high-decibel polemics—the anti-Brown counterpart of the work of James Redpath. As it turned out, Mrs. Sara T. Robinson, whose late husband and one-time governor of Kansas had challenged the Brown legend as presented in the hero-worshipping biographies, had commissioned Wilson to write a book that would "reverse" Villard's favorable portrait of Brown "in Kansas and afterwards." She offered Wilson $5,000 to do the job, but died without paying up. He had to sue her heirs to get his money. Those sympathetic to Brown, of course, castigated Wilson.

* Sanborn, for example, wrote that Villard's biography "is useful for some facts which do not appear elsewhere, but is vitiated by a false estimate of Brown's character, which leads him to make foolish guesses instead of giving the facts as they were."

"The would-be historian who sells himself for such a person trebly prostitutes his powers," wrote Villard; "he is untrue to himself, to his state, and to our mistress, History." Later, James C. Malin, who also wrote to deflate the Brown legend, claimed that Wilson had arrived at his views before Mrs. Robinson approached him. If so, that still does not alter what the book is: an anti-Brown tract that will always be enjoyed, as C. B. Galbreath put it, "by the critically inclined who place a low estimate upon humanitarian endeavor and reluctantly accord unselfish motives to others."

In the South, a counterlegend had grown up about John Brown, but no full-scale biography that argued the Southern view existed until Robert Penn Warren, a native of Kentucky, published *John Brown, the Making of a Martyr*, in 1929. Eschewing original research in manuscript sources, Warren borrowed his facts from Sanborn and Villard in order to construct a case against Brown and his abolitionist supporters and followers. Flippant, condescending, and contemptuous of Brown throughout his volume, Warren described him as an inept and warped Yankee businessman who became a violent abolitionist fanatic. The central trait of Brown's personality, Warren suggested, was his genius at rationalizing his faults and failures, a genius glaringly evident when he posed as a saint during his trial and execution. "It was all so thin," Warren observed, "that it should not have deceived a child, but it deceived a generation." In Warren's opinion, Brown was a criminal whose only virtue was his courage—the same opinion that Edmund Ruffin, the Virginia secessionist, had expressed after Brown's execution. Warren's interpretation was so partisan that even Avery Craven, who was himself sympathetic toward the Southern point of view, found it "an indictment, not an unbiased biography."

IV

Except for Du Bois, no professional historian had thus far produced a book-length treatment of Brown, one based on exhaustive research and imbued with an objective and critical spirit. In 1942, James C. Malin, professor of history at the University of Kansas, published a volume that claimed to perform this laudable task, that purported to make "a scientific study" of Brown by applying "to the problem in full measure the critical technique of modern historiography." In reality, despite its wealth of detail and its demolition of many myths, Malin's *John Brown and the Legend of Fifty-Six* was not a scientific study but a partisan work of the anti-Brown school. Malin based his 794-page volume almost exclusively on holdings in the Kansas State Historical Society, ignoring (or using in only a limited manner) indispensable Brown materials in various other libraries and repositories. But the least scientific feature of Malin's book was its biased portrait of Brown himself. Commencing with an examination of Brown's pre-Kansas career, Malin argued that Brown was a restless and dishonest speculator. He insisted that "two or more" of Brown's many business ventures involved "crime" (Malin did not specify which ventures) and that Brown's "flagrant dishonesty" in both his business and family relations made him unreliable as a character witness. Accepting only four "authentic episodes" in which Brown was connected with "the negro question," Malin concluded that Brown's views and activities did not "differ materially from those of any number of the active anti-slavery or abolitionist people of the time."

Since these points provide the foundation for Malin's thesis, they deserve careful examination. First, while Malin rightly rejected the myth that all Brown had ever been interested in was overthrowing slavery by the sword, his contention that Brown was merely another abolitionist hardly did him justice. A Calvinist and a stubborn nonconformist, he had refused to join any antislavery organization and argued with his abolitionist acquaintances about their religious convictions, especially those who believed in free will and the perfectibility of man. Moreover, from 1847 to 1855 Brown became increasingly belligerent, rejecting the doctrines of both the political abolitionists and the nonresistant Garrisonians and advocating a policy of violent opposition to the aggressions of the "Slave Power." Furthermore, what about Brown's friendship with Frederick Douglass? And what about the Subterranean Pass Way scheme? Malin not only refused even to bring up the latter project for analysis (either to accept or reject it), but also dismissed Brown's involvement with Douglass as not "particularly important"—although the Negro leader viewed Brown as one of the most forceful and extraordinary white abolitionists he had met. After visiting Brown in late 1847 and hearing the details of the Subterranean Pass Way scheme, Douglass wrote the *North Star* that he had had "a private interview" with Brown, who, "though a white gentleman, is in sympathy, a black man, and as deeply interested in our cause, as though his own soul had been pierced with the iron of slavery." Brown, for his part, could scarcely restrain his joy at finding black men like Douglass—men who "possessed the energy of head and heart to demand freedom for their whole people." The result would be—must be—"the downfall of slavery." Douglass visited Brown again in 1848. And in the months that followed, his own antislavery utterances "became more and more tinged by the color of this man's strong impressions." At an abolitionist convention at Salem, Ohio, Douglass repeated what Brown had told him and said he feared that only bloodshed could annihilate slavery now.

Second, Malin's contention that Brown's business activities before he went to Kansas involved "crime" and "flagrant dishonesty" was unfairly slanted. True, Brown had a talent for overstatement and exaggeration, especially when he was excited. But he could also be scrupulously and commendably honest. It is a fact that in 1838 he took money a New England wool company had entrusted to him and used it to pay his private debts. Yet the company did not press charges, and Brown vowed—and seriously attempted—to pay the money back, until forced into bankruptcy in 1842. Moreover, when Brown opened a wool agency in Springfield, Massachusetts, he pledged part of his commission toward paying this and other debts. While most of his business deals did end in disaster and while he was plagued with endless litigation for not meeting his obligations and settling his debts, few if any of the businessmen who took him to court accused him of crime or "flagrant dishonesty." Rather, they accused him of being negligent, careless, and inept.

Malin's account of Brown in Kansas is equally one-sided—an elaboration on the theme of the restless and dishonest speculator. If Brown was an unscrupulous operator with only an ordinary interest in slavery, it followed that he could never have been genuinely concerned with the free-state cause in the Territory. Thus Malin insisted that Brown set out for Kansas, in a wagon loaded down with guns and swords, only to find a business deal! This assertion not only ignored Brown's fighting temperament, but dismissed John Jr.'s letters of June 22 and 29, 1855, which reported that business opportunities were not at all promising in Kansas.

Although Malin actually quoted John Jr. to that effect, he proceeded to ignore the very quotation in asserting that Brown migrated to the Territory for purposes of business and settlement. In the letter of June 29 (which Malin either dismissed or never read), John Jr. also declared in his most impassioned prose that a great war was about to erupt between free-state and proslavery partisans in Kansas and again pleaded with his father to bring guns with him. Malin to the contrary, it would seem that Brown himself most accurately described his ultimate reason for going to the Territory. "Four of my sons had gone there to settle, and they induced me to go," he told a retinue of interrogators after Harpers Ferry. "I did not go there to settle, but because of the difficulties."

In Malin's opinion, Brown became involved in the difficulties in Kansas after he arrived there, not because he hated slavery and its Missouri and Kansas defenders, or because he thought their efforts to force slavery on Kansas were unjust and a sin against God, but because the struggle brought out his basic criminal nature and afforded him an opportunity to steal horses (which was Wilson's thesis). Rejecting a considerable body of evidence to the contrary, Malin argued that all the threats of murder and annihilation issued by proslavery forces had no impact on Brown, that enemy atrocities did not disturb him either, and that he instigated the Pottawatomie massacre largely for political reasons. According to Malin, Brown selected his victims for two reasons: because they had been associated with Cato's proslavery court when it sat in session at Pottawatomie Creek, and because they were going to testify against Brown at the Lykins County session of the court, to open on May 26, 1856, on a charge of treasonably resisting the proslavery territorial government. Yet Malin conceded that there was a problem with his interpretation: Brown had spared the life of James Harris, who had also been a juror on Cato's court. "If the assassination was directed at those who participated in the court, why was he permitted to go free?"

Malin did not answer his own question. Nor did he address himself to other problems his thesis contained. For one thing, since neither Brown nor any of his sons had been indicted at the Pottawatomie session of Cato's court, why should Brown have been preoccupied with the personnel of the court? Why indeed did Brown allow Harris, as well as other members of the proslavery court who resided on the creek, to live? Most likely he did so because they had not actively aided Missouri intruders or threatened their free-state neighbors, as the victims evidently had done. Furthermore, Malin gave no evidence that Brown knew he was going to be indicted for treason by the court when it opened in Lykins County (I could find no such evidence either). And even if Brown had known, would he have cared? Although the Cato court had indicted several free-state men for crimes and misdemeanors, no attempt had been made to arrest them. And if it was feared that arrests might be made this time, why didn't John Jr. and some of the others who had resisted the laws (and who were subsequently indicted by the court on treason charges) accompany Brown on the massacre? Because of these unanswered questions, the political assassination theory would hardly seem a plausible explanation of the massacre. While the exact motives that prompted Brown to kill those men may never be known, I am inclined to accept the "retaliatory blow" thesis—that Brown instigated the murders both to avenge proslavery atrocities (the killing of six free-state men, the sacking of Lawrence) and to create "a restraining fear." He wished to show "by actual work" that he was one free-state partisan who was not afraid to fight back. The retaliatory blow thesis seems to fit the logic of events and Brown's own behavior during the sack of Lawrence better than any other explanation given for the Pottawatomie killings.

Perhaps bothered by his own interpretation, Malin wrote elsewhere in his volume that Brown may also have had some devious psychological purpose for perpetrating the murders. Since John Jr. (who commanded the Pottawatomie column that marched to the defense of Lawrence) had overruled Brown "on all points relative to the expedition," the massacre may have been in part "the explosive self-assertion of a frustrated old man . . . a means by which he might enjoy untrammelled authority and restore his confidence in himself."

Malin accepted Wilson's thesis that, in the civil war of 1856, Brown used the free-state cause as a cloak to steal the horses and property of "innocent settlers." In truth, Brown did steal horses from proslavery people—proslavery partisans also stole horses from free-state people. Yet plundering and horse stealing were perfectly justifiable in Brown's mind, because he believed that he was waging a holy war against obstinately wicked men. His letters contained telling references to God, "who has not given us over to the will of our enemies but has moreover delivered them into our hands" and who "will we humbly trust still keep & deliver us." Anyway, "a state of war existed," as one of Brown's recruits asserted, "and it was quite proper to despoil the enemy." Yet there is no evidence that he kept the money made from the sale of horses for his personal gain. On the contrary, he used the money and stolen supplies "for the continuation of the struggle."

As for Brown's importance in the Kansas civil war, Malin contended that an analysis of contemporary sources—especially proslavery newspapers—suggested that Brown did little in either "making or marring Kansas history." He was never a major factor; his exploits were eruptions of disorder that had no relationship with either radical or conservative free-state strategy. Thus, destroying Brown as no other writer had ever done, Malin described him as "no more outstanding as a villain than as a hero." Malin, of course, is entitled to his opinion. But it would be fairer to say that Brown was simply not an organization man; a nonconformist all his adult life, he refused to take orders from conservative, "broken-down" politicians like Charles Robinson who, in Brown's judgment, were afraid to fight. The old man elected to wage his own private war, in his own way, against the proslavery enemy. And he *did* fight—at Black Jack, at Sugar Creek, and at Osawatomie. Consequently, he *was* in Kansas history and cannot be dismissed, as Malin himself had to concede. Moreover, Brown's experiences in Bleeding Kansas convinced him that he should expand his war against the South, that God, who remained an "*all powerful*" directive force in Brown's life, wished him to do so. When fighting in Kansas seemed at an end in 1857, he conceived his Virginia plan to attack slavery directly. And in this respect the significance of Brown in Kansas takes on an added dimension of importance which has been too little emphasized.

Was Brown crazy? Malin suggested that he was, using as evidence a letter written in 1859 by C. G. Allen, a Christian minister, who recalled that he had heard several persons say that they thought Old Brown was "insane" after the battle of Osawatomie. Malin pronounced this "a damaging piece of evidence," although in his analysis of the Pottawatomie massacre and the growth of the Brown legend, he repeatedly attacked pro-Brown writers for using hearsay evidence.

As for Brown's career after the Kansas civil war, Malin agreed with Wilson that Brown turned to his Harpers Ferry plan less to free the slaves than to loot and plunder on a grand scale in the South itself. While Brown failed in this enterprise, he nevertheless "possessed a capacity for self-justification for his failures which amounted almost to genius [Warren's thesis], and on his final rôle he staked his claims to immortality and worked himself to a state of religious immolation." Although religion was the guiding force of Brown's life, this was the only time Malin discussed the subject in his entire study.

Thus far I have concentrated on Malin's conception of Brown and have said little about the merits of his work. Malin reappraised Brown's role in both the Wakarusa War and in the last defense of Lawrence in September 1856, pointing out that Villard overstated Brown's importance in those events. Malin also gave a valuable account of the organization of the proslavery court system and of the activities of the Hoogland Commission in the summer of 1856. In addition, he demonstrated that the struggle between proslavery and free-state men was not always over slavery, but sometimes involved conflicting land claims. Malin provided a helpful analysis of free-state and proslavery newspapers and included an assessment of the growth of John Brown historiography from Redpath to Robert Penn Warren, showing how some of the principals in the Brown controversy—Sanborn and Robinson among them—changed positions regarding the Pottawatomie massacre. Yet *John Brown and the Legend of Fifty-Six* was essentially a biased and one-sided study of Brown the man. And this was especially unfortunate in view of the large number of historians who accepted Malin's interpretation as a "scientific" one.*

V

If Malin's conception of Brown found wide acceptance among historians, so did the case study of Brown that Allan Nevins in-

* Wrote David M. Potter: "James C. Malin . . . has applied the rigorous pruning hook of historical method to the luxuriant growth of unsupported assertion about John Brown in Kansas. The residue of fact which remains presents such startling contrasts to the legend that Malin's study has value, apart from the Kansas question, as a case study in historical method." Potter, *The South and the Sectional Conflict* (Baton Rouge, La., 1968), 140.

cluded in volume 2 of *The Emergence of Lincoln.* Indeed, the views of Malin and Nevins in large part became the conventional wisdom about Brown in the historical profession. Although Nevins's study contained brilliant insights into the Harpers Ferry attack and revealed more of the contradictions and complexities of Brown's personality than any of the works discussed thus far, the account was marred by numerous errors and a highly questionable approach.* For Nevins insisted on psychoanalyzing Brown largely on the basis of partisan testimony given nearly a century before. In diagnosing Brown's "mental disease," his "psychogenic malady," Nevins maintained that Brown, partly from his inheritance and partly from a lifetime of sickness and hardship, was suffering from "reasoning insanity" or "ambitious paranoia," a mental disease characterized by "systematized delusions." It is significant that of all the extremists (Southern racists and fire-eaters included) described in *The Emergence of Lincoln,* Brown was the only one Nevins psychoanalyzed. To be sure, his diagnosis only reinforced what Brown's detractors had said all along—the man was crazy. And because he was crazy, it was not necessary to understand him in the context of the problems and paradoxes of American society that helped bring him to Harpers Ferry. Once again, this "stone in the historians' shoe," as Truman Nelson phrased it, could be conveniently dismissed as a madman.

I do not suggest, of course, that the historian has nothing to learn from psychology and what it has discovered about human

---

* Everybody makes mistakes, of course, but there seems an unusual number in Nevins's account of Brown. Among them: Brown's business associates did not "rue" their partnerships with him. Brown's mother did not die insane. The League of Gileadites was formed in 1851, not 1850. Brown did not lose his reputation for probity during his business disasters of 1837–1841 (Heman Oviatt, Seth Thompson, and Simon Perkins all formed partnerships with him afterwards). Brown did not relocate in North Elba, New York, and then see his sons off to Kansas. He saw them off before he moved east. Brown was not so much a "cranky skeptic" about Christ and the New Testament as he was a Calvinist who rooted his theology in the Old Testament. One may not "question the sanity of a nearly penniless man with a large family who devotes a month" to writing a letter of exhortation to John Jr. regarding his religious views. Brown wrote some of the letter, then waited a month before he came back to finish it. Equally wrong is the assertion that Brown, in the letters he wrote in 1859, "makes but one reference to Christ, and none to Christian mercy." In fact, Brown made at least seven major references to Jesus in his prison letters, and exhorted his children both to hate slavery and to do good and help the poor.

behavior. As Paul Murray Kendall said, "Psychology and psycho-analysis have thrust fingers of light into the cave of the human mind, have deepened our sense of the complexities, the arcane tides, of personality, have enabled us to penetrate some of the dark corners of motive and desire, to detect patterns of action, and sense the symbolic value of word and gesture." Still, it is one thing to learn from what psychology has taught us about human beings. It is quite another for the historian to assume the role of the psychiatrist, as Nevins did with Brown, and to persist in diagnosing the "mental disease" of some long-dead historical figure whose hidden anxieties and inner conflicts cannot be probed in psychiatric sessions. One may doubt whether many responsible psychiatrists today would want to analyze the troubles of their patients strictly on the basis of their letters and what others (friends and enemies alike) have said about them. Furthermore, history is already imprecise enough without intruding on it all the recondite terminology, controversies and disagreements, of yet another imprecise discipline. The historian who does that is likely to confuse the very issues he seeks to clarify and understand.

If one can question the validity of Nevins's clinical approach, one can also criticize much of the evidence used to support it. He not only referred to Brown's "deluded," "irrational" behavior during the genesis and execution of his raid and ensuing trial, but also placed heavy reliance on nineteen affidavits that were given by Brown's friends and relatives shortly after he was sentenced to hang. These documents claimed that insanity ran in the maternal side of the family and that Brown himself suffered from mental disorders. Drawing on these documents as his evidence, Nevins asserted that Brown inherited part of his mental aberrations from his mother, Ruth Mills Brown, who, "like his maternal grandmother, died insane." Not only does this statement ignore the whole question as to whether or not mental aberrations can be inherited, it is also inaccurate. There is no evidence that Brown's mother was ever insane. None of the affidavits claimed that she had been insane or peculiar in any way. Thus, if one insists on arguing that Brown labored from "hereditary insanity," one must rest one's case on the assumption that his disorders came from his grandmother. And there is no evidence at all as to what her problem was. True, the affidavits claimed that she was insane, but that is of little help to us: the word insanity is a vague, emotion-charged, and clinically meaningless term. Even in a historical context, as C. Vann Woodward reminded us, the term is misleading, ambiguous, and relative—it has meant different things to different people in the past, and what seems insane in one period may seem perfectly sane at other times.* Even in nineteenth-century parlance, insanity was a catch-all term used to describe a wide range of odd or unacceptable behavior. Therefore, when the affiants speak of the insanity of Brown's grandmother, we do not know what sort of disorder they were describing. Maybe she was just senile.

The affiants also stated that many of Brown's uncles, aunts, and cousins on his mother's side were insane, that his only sister and his brother Salmon were insane or said to be insane, that his first wife Dianthe and two of their sons—John Jr. and Frederick —had exhibited symptoms, and that Brown, too, was mentally disturbed, although opinions varied as to the nature and source of his affliction. Biographers and historians must beware of using these claims as clinical evidence. As Louis Ruchames noted, the affidavits contained a great deal of information based not on direct knowledge of the cases they described, but on hearsay (as Sylvester Thompson admitted). In the case of Brown's immediate family, there is no evidence that Salmon Brown, who was the editor of the New Orleans *Bee*, was insane. As for Brown's sons, if one accepts the assumption that mental troubles can be hereditary, then one must face the argument that both sons inherited their difficulties from Dianthe, not Brown. Actually a much more plausible explanation is that John Jr.'s depression and melancholia resulted from his experiences in Kansas: the haggling with his father as to what they should do during the Lawrence crisis, the tension and lack of sleep, the humiliation he had suffered when his political friends turned against him after the Pottawatomie massacre, and the cruel treatment he received at the hands of U.S. troops following his capture. And what of Frederick? If we may believe Samuel Adair, Brown's preacher brother-in-law, Frederick was suffering from what doctors at that time diagnosed as "an

* In *The Burden of Southern History* (revised ed., New York, 1968), 43–44, C. Vann Woodward warns us to be careful in approaching the insanity question, because it can blind us to the meaning of Harpers Ferry and confuse the whole issue. Then he proceeds to confuse the issue by accepting those controversial affidavits at their face value.

accumulation of blood on the brain" that caused "blinding head-aches" and left him temporarily incoherent and "flighty." He could have had a brain tumor. Or perhaps his trouble was epilepsy.

Finally—and this is a crucial point—the affidavits were intended above all to save Brown's life, by convincing Governor Henry A. Wise and the state of Virginia that Brown was insane, that he was not responsible for his acts, and that he should be placed in an asylum. The documents were not objective clinical evidence gathered by doctors who wanted to establish as clearly as possible what Brown's mental disorders were. When the affiants asserted that Brown was insane, they were giving their opinions for a partisan objective. Although many of them doubtlessly believed that their opinions were true, they were still opinions. Except for Dr. Jonathan Metcalf of Hudson, Ohio, none of the affiants was educated in medical matters, and none of them was a psychologist.

All this is not to go to the other extreme and argue that Brown was a normal, sane, well-adjusted individual. These terms are meaningless, too. That Brown was a revolutionary who believed himself called by God to purge this land with blood, that he had an excitable temperament and could get carried away with one idea, that he was inept, egotistical, hard on his sons, afflicted with chronic attacks of the ague, and worn down from a lifetime of hardship, that he could have five men he regarded as his enemies assassinated with broadswords, and that he wanted to become either an American Spartacus at the head of a slave army or a martyred soldier who was the first to die in a sectional war over slavery—all this is true. Yet Brown could also be kind and gentle —extremely gentle. He could rock a baby lamb in his arms. He could stay up several nights caring for a sick child, or his ailing father, or his afflicted first wife. He could hold children on both knees and sing them the sad, melancholy refrains of "Blow ye the trumpet, blow." He could stand at the graves of four of his children who had died of dysentery, weeping and praising God in an ecstasy of despair. He could teach his children to fear God and keep the Commandments—and exhibit the most excruciating anxiety when they began questioning the value of religion. He could treat Negroes as his fellow human beings, inviting them to eat at his family table and addressing his black workers as "Mr."— a trait that cannot be praised enough, in view of the anti-Negro prejudice that prevailed among most Northerners and nearly all Southerners in his time. He could offer to take a Negro child into his home, could dream for years of establishing a Negro school, could move his family to the Adirondack Mountains in upstate New York to help a Negro community there, and could deplore racial discrimination in Ohio, especially in the churches. And he could feel an almost paralyzing bitterness toward slavery itself and all the people in the United States who sought to preserve and protect it. Thus to label Brown as an insane man—even a reasoning insane man—is to disregard or minimize the more favorable traits of his personality, especially his sympathy for the suffering of black people in the United States. And it is to ignore the piercing insight he had into what his raid might do to sectional tensions that already existed. Nor can John Brown be removed from the context of the violent, irrational, and paradoxical times in which he lived. A man of "powerful religious convictions" who believed to his bones that slavery was a sin against God, he was profoundly distressed that a nation which claimed to be both Christian and free should condone, protect, and perpetuate that "sum of villanies." It was not only his angry, messianic mind, but the racist, slave society in which he lived—one that professed "under God" to provide liberty and justice for all—that helped bring John Brown to Harpers Ferry.

VI

Except for a few scholars like Benjamin Quarles, whose *Allies for Freedom* (1974) is a perceptive and fair-minded study of Brown's ties with black Americans, historians today continue to embrace the views of Malin and Nevins as correct.* As a consequence, highly charged labels like "psychopath," "grim, terrible fanatic," "at the last a monomaniac," still infest the literature that touches on the Brown problem. In *Race and Politics: "Bleeding Kansas" and the Coming of the Civil War* (1969), James A. Rawley describes Brown as a deranged man "with insanity in his ancestry,"

* Albert Fried's *John Brown's Journey: Notes and Reflections on his America and Mine* (1978), which is sympathetic to Brown, came out while *Our Fiery Trial* was in press. For a discussion of Fried's work, see the reference notes to this chapter.

a criminal "deserving of execration instead of exaltation." Monroe Lee Billington, in *The American South* (1971), derides Harpers Ferry as "the misguided act of a madman," and William R. Brock, in *Conflict and Transformation* (1973), agrees that Brown was "a man of unstable temperament" and "violent determination." David Potter, in *The Impending Crisis* (1976), dismisses the influence of Brown's intense Calvinism on the Harpers Ferry attack, ignores Brown's burning conviction that his raid would cause a sectional upheaval even if it failed, and questions Brown's mental stability, referring to the mental troubles in his family and citing both Nevins and Vann Woodward regarding Brown's psychological makeup. In *Division and Reunion: America, 1848–1877* (1978), Ludwell H. Johnson brazenly asserts that Brown was a cattle-rustling, horse-stealing desperado whose weird and wicked deeds "settled the question" of his sanity. In *Roll, Jordan, Roll* (1974), Marxist historian Eugene D. Genovese pronounces Brown "fanatical, millenarian, and possibly mad." Writes Genovese: "What judgment should be rendered on a society the evils of which reach such proportions that only madmen are sane enough to challenge them?" One could well ask what judgment should be rendered on a Marxist historian who categorizes Brown as mad but who finds nothing at all insane about George Fitzhugh, the subject of one of Genovese's earlier studies, who wanted to enslave whites and blacks alike and haul the world back to feudalism? Moreover, what judgment should be rendered on David Donald, who, in the latest edition of *The Civil War and Reconstruction* (1969), judges Harpers Ferry "an insane attack" and denigrates Brown himself as "a grim, terrible man" whose mental condition is "that of obsession and extreme, unbalanced fanaticism"? Yet in *Charles Sumner and the Coming of the Civil War* (1960), Donald excuses Preston Brooks's violent beating of Sumner in 1856, explaining only that Brooks had "a smoldering hatred of abolitionists, a proud devotion to the South and to South Carolina, an intense loyalty to his family, and a determination to live by the code of a gentleman."

If anti-Brown prejudice still flourishes in the community of historians, it inhabits the larger world as well. In 1975 the National Endowment for the Humanities refused to fund a projected public television series on Brown, declaring that the proposal did not properly vilify the man as a violent devil whose Harpers Ferry enterprise "made no sense at all." The Director of Public Programs hastened to point out that the N.E.H. had been fully advised, not only by "several independent experts on Brown," but by a panel of humanities scholars, professional filmmakers, and "distinguished private citizens." According to the Director of Public Programs, these reviewers held that Stephen B. Oates, whose writings on Brown had influenced those who proposed the television series, was one of the few historians in the field who had dedicated himself "to whitewashing John Brown."

FOUR

MODERN RADICALS AND JOHN BROWN

I<small>T</small> is commonplace for Ameri-
can activists—like activists everywhere else—to use history for
self-vindication. Too many of them regard the past as a rich store-
house of banners and slogans, all proclaiming some great moral
lesson that justifies their particular cause or party line. Southern
white supremacists, in their fight against "forced integration,"
cite the Bible to defend segregation, wave Confederate battle flags,
and declaim the old Lost Cause shibboleths of state's rights and
freedom of choice. Conservative Republicans, as I discuss in a
subsequent essay, invoke the hackneyed lessons of the American
frontier to rally support for their crusade against liberal Democrats and government welfare. And liberal Democrats like Walt
Rostow still rehearse the example of Munich—which "teaches
us" the futility of appeasement—to defend American involvement
in Vietnam.

Conservatives and liberals, though, are not the only American
advocates who use history for political ends. White and black
radicals do it too. By radicals I mean those who are attempting to
bring about revolutionary changes in American society, in order
to eradicate such institutionalized wrongs as racist and sexist oppression, moral hypocrisies, police brutality, capitalist exploita-
tion, and imperialistic wars. Still, radicals can no more break with
the past than can liberals, conservatives, or reactionaries. For
radicals too must have historical heroes. They too must find grand
examples that sanctify their views and ennoble their cause, making them feel part of an eternal struggle against injustice.

So it is with those radicals who canonize John Brown of Harpers

Ferry. For those fighting against racial oppression in our time, Brown is the great ancestor, to be memorialized and enshrined. Consequently he is depicted in radical sources—in histories, essays, and novels—as an immortal soldier of freedom whom today's black and white children should idolize. He is defended, too, from "racist" biographies which ascribe human error and human weaknesses to him. As a result, a modern radical mythology now flourishes about John Brown, one that merits meticulous comparison to the actual historical record. For such a critique may reveal a great deal about how history can be transformed into hagiography and utilized as symbol and shibboleth for modern causes.

The legend of Brown as immortal hero actually began in November and December of 1859, when the abolitionists extolled him as an American saint. A long procession of reverential biographies, poems, and novels perpetuated the legend from 1860 down to the last half of the twentieth century, when some civil rights advocates found Brown an appropriate symbol for their own struggles against injustice. For the late Louis Ruchames, scholar of the abolitionist movement and staunch supporter of Negro rights in our time, Brown represented "the highest ideals of equality and democracy" and "the best in the Judaeo-Christian tradition." Even though Brown directed the Pottawatomie killings and tried to incite a slave insurrection at Harpers Ferry, Ruchames still thought him a suitable hero for today's nonviolent civil rights movement. More recently, Herbert Aptheker has argued that Brown is an apt hero for all of today's blacks—especially the children, who need a great man like him to emulate. On that score, Aptheker insists that the best book for them to read is Du Bois's *John Brown*, which glorifies the Old Hero as an enduring symbol of right against wrong.

While several advocates in recent years have mythologized Brown, the most complete and most impassioned canonization has come from the pen of Truman Nelson, historical novelist, polemicist, and radical white anarchist who champions the black liberation movement in its ongoing fight against white racism. Nelson's conception of Brown is dramatized in his long novel, *The Surveyor* (1960), an account of Brown as superhero in Bleeding Kansas. But Nelson's view is most emphatically stated in his essays for the *Nation*—"John Brown Revisited" (1957) and "You Have Not Studied Them Right" (1971)—and in his semifictional polemic,

The Old Man: John Brown at Harper's Ferry (1973). In his writings, Nelson argues that his Hero was not only an unswerving Friend of Man, but a tough-minded anarchist, a bold, opportunistic, olympian revolutionary who, instead of trying to incite an insurrection at Harpers Ferry, pulled off "a classic coup" which led ultimately to "the final victory at Appomattox." Conceding that Brown told lies to achieve his ends ("He was, in the naive argot of the scholars, 'mendacious' to the very end"), Nelson asserts that his deeds "can be now considered ethically compatible with actions and tactics familiar to revolutionary guerrilla warfare and liberating resistance movements." A prototype of those currently involved in such movements, Brown acted not from "a narrow sense of sin," but from "a great liberating, friend to man principle." Because Brown bears "a strikingly close relationship to the revolutionary mood prevailing today," Nelson can write about him only with "love and awe." And those who cannot—those writers and scholars who "malign" Brown by citing his unfavorable as well as his positive traits—ought in Nelson's opinion to undergo sensitivity training. Maybe then they will stop their "spurious balancing off." Maybe then they will cease destroying the minds of their students "through a printed circuit of derevolutionizing and deprinciplizing interpretations." Maybe then they will recognize John Brown as "a great man, a great soul, a great humanitarian and abolitionist."

In so deifying Brown, Nelson is speaking for a great many black and white advocates—and that includes teachers, students, writers, and editors as well as lecture-circuit orators. And it is this deification of Brown, this glorification of him as a set-piece hero for modern radicals, that deeply concerns me both as a historian and a humanist. While Brown *was* a bold, imposing, high-minded individual and while he *did* detest the evils of racial slavery, most of Nelson's didactic interpretation wrenches Brown out of historical context until he is no longer the Calvinist insurrectionary of 1859, but a full-blown, modern-day secular revolutionary—and a saintly one at that. Although the historical record discloses that Brown was a self-styled religious prophet, a man who felt it his divine mission to free the slaves, Nelson absolutely denies that Brown was a Calvinist. Nelson is preoccupied with this point, perhaps because he resides in Massachusetts and equates all Calvinists with the Puritan witch-hunters of colonial Massachusetts

Bay. "Brown was no Calvinist bigot," Nelson writes, and assails any biographer who attempts to identify Brown with Calvinist theology. On this score, Nelson contends that only a revolutionary like himself can understand another revolutionary. He insists that Brown was not even religious, arguing that the Old Hero stopped attending church in middle age and that he merely used the Bible —as did other rebels in history—to find precedents for revolution. While Nelson concedes that Brown had some people killed in Kansas and that he raided Harpers Ferry (where seventeen people died), he nevertheless insists that the old man was not a *violent* revolutionary, but a *loving* one. Because love, says Nelson, is what revolution is all about . . . although Nelson contradicts himself in his own manifesto, *The Right of Revolution* (1968), which urges violent resistance against America's white racist society and which quotes liberally from and about John Brown.

Nelson's image of Brown is romantic nonsense, for the evidence that Brown was both a Calvinist and a violent revolutionary is massive and irrefutable. Yet, in saying this, I am not condemning Nelson or the black liberation movement he defends, because as a historian I see profound similarities between the racially troubled America that has produced today's black militants and the turbulent, slaveholding America that spawned John Brown. What I am saying is that Nelson's inflexible revolutionary ideology explains the distorted view that he and other contemporary radicals have of Brown as a man. It is imperative for Nelson to see Brown as he sees himself, to impose *his* values and *his* beliefs onto that prodigious figure of antebellum America, because it gives Nelson a sense of historical rightness he could not otherwise have. Therefore, since Nelson and today's radicals are not Calvinists, Brown was not a Calvinist. Never mind the testimony of his family, his friends, his employees, and his abolitionist sponsors that he was "a Puritan of the Old Order." Never mind that Brown himself expressed a belief in an implacable and sovereign God in most of the letters he wrote from about 1830 until he was hanged in 1859. Never mind the fact that a man can be a dedicated Christian and still not attend church, especially if he believes—as Brown did— that the Church is bigoted and proslavery. Truman Nelson is not religious. Brown was not religious. And woe indeed to anybody who says differently.

If Nelson ignores the evidence about Brown's religious beliefs, he likewise distorts Brown's record as an antislavery militant. Certainly the man was capable of "consummate acts of love," as Nelson argues, but the evidence proves beyond doubt that he was also a truculent individual, intolerant of others, deaf to criticism, and obsessed with wickedness—especially the wickedness of "Southern slavocrats." Frederick Douglass claimed that Brown was enraged at Southerners and was perfectly willing to spill blood should they prevent him from running slaves into the North. Brown also chided Negroes for passively submitting to white oppression and befriended black militants like Henry Highland Garnet, who had actually called on the slaves to revolt. In 1851 Brown exhorted Negroes to kill any Southerner or federal officer who tried to enforce the Fugitive Slave Law, and he enlisted forty-four blacks from Springfield, Massachusetts, in a mutual-defense organization called the Branch of the U.S. League of Gileadites, based on the story of Gideon in the Book of Judges.

Later, in all the hysteria and violence in Kansas, Brown conceived and supervised the night-time assassinations of five proslavery settlers on Pottawatomie Creek. Anti-Brown writers have labeled him a homicidal maniac for these slayings, ignoring the fact that proslavery forces had already murdered six free-state men in cold blood and had threatened to exterminate every "Goddamned Abolitionist" in the Territory. In the context of all the violence and threats of annihilation that prevailed in Kansas, one can understand why a man of Brown's temperament might be driven to commit the Pottawatomie killings as "a retaliatory blow" to create "a restraining fear." But let us be honest about Brown's motivations: it was not love but hatred that impelled him to kill those men on the Pottawatomie. He hated anybody who advocated the ownership of another human being. He hated the proslavery Missourians, who had invaded Kansas, voted illegally in elections there, bushwhacked free-state settlers, and burned the town of Lawrence. He hated Southern slaveowners because their *"hellish"* institution was monstrously cruel to black people and made a mockery of God's law and the Declaration of Independence. His letters throughout the 1850s are filled not only with love for his family and for his black and white friends, but with profound moral outrage against Southern slaveowners and all their Northern chums and allies. Finally, after years of accumulated rage, unable to stand any more proslavery atrocities, excited to a frenzy over the sack of Lawrence, he surrendered himself to violence by the sword.

I wish that Nelson—and everybody else who views Brown as a saint—would examine his letters and all other documents relating to the Pottawatomie massacre (particularly the testimony of eyewitnesses) with an open mind. I wish they would do the same with the historical evidence about the Harpers Ferry raid, an operation that Nelson for his part persists in misrepresenting. He misrepresents both the scope and the objectives of the attack, entirely dismissing its more grisly aspects in order to present his hero in the best possible light. Elaborating on his argument that Brown was a man of love and not of hate, Nelson states that the Old Hero never intended to incite a general slave insurrection in the South. Instead, he "planned a very localized operation" in northern Virginia, one that might be gradually expanded through "planned warfare" should there be enough forces available to carry it out. True, Brown talked about the possibility of a purely defensive operation (much depended, after all, on what kind of opposition he encountered). But there is a large and persuasive body of evidence that his plans called for something far larger than the innocent little enterprise Nelson suggests. Brown's son Salmon contended that the old man hoped either to incite an insurrection or to cause a major sectional crisis that would result in the death of slavery. "The Harpers Ferry raid had that idea behind it far more than any other," Salmon claimed. At the 1858 convention at Chatham, Canada, where Brown perfected the Harpers Ferry scheme, he outlined to a group of black and white allies how he planned to incite a Southern-wide slave revolt. In a provisional constitution adopted at Chatham, he declared war on slavery, which itself was "a most barbarous, unprovoked, and unjustifiable War" against Negroes, and proposed to establish a revolutionary black state in the Southern mountains. At the same time, he told his clandestine abolitionist backers—the Secret Six —that if the insurrection began and held its ground even for a few days, "the whole country from the Potomac to Savannah would be ablaze." He compiled a list of Southern towns, from Florida to Texas, that contained federal forts or arsenals whose weapons he desperately needed for the full-scale uprising he hoped to instigate. He argued that his mere presence in the South would cause spontaneous slave insurrections in all directions; and he worked over maps of the Southern states, drawing circled crosses on those counties and towns where slaves outnumbered whites and where slave uprisings would likely occur. "If I could conquer Virginia," he explained later, "the balance of the Southern states would nearly conquer themselves, there being such a large number of slaves in them." William Leeman, one of Brown's recruits, wrote his mother on the eve of the raid: "We are now all privately gathered in a slave state, where we are determined to strike for freedom, incite the slaves to rebellion, and establish a free government." Brown was quite prepared to plunge the entire nation into civil war, because he had repeatedly said to his friends and backers —to George Luther Stearns, Franklin Sanborn, James Hanway, and Ralph Waldo Emerson—that it was better that "a whole generation of men, women, and children should pass away by violent death" than for slavery to endure in the United States.

Moreover, Brown profoundly believed that he was guided by *"an all good, all wise, & all powerful"* God—his letters ring with such statements—and that it was this God who was directing the entire Harpers Ferry enterprise. However difficult it is for people in our secular age to accept Brown's intense religious beliefs, he nevertheless thought himself an instrument in the hands of an angry God. He was a full-fledged warrior of the Old Testament now. He was "like David of old." He was like Gideon, who, guided by Jehovah himself, attacked the Midianites and drove them across Jordan. He was like Samson who single-handedly pulled the temple down. As a soldier of the Almighty, called to punish this nation for its sins, Brown was certain that God would use him and his raid for His own designs.

When the raid failed and Brown came to trial in Charleston, he concluded that the Almighty now wanted to use Harpers Ferry for another purpose. And that was to arouse the North by having Brown crucified on the gallows. "I can trust God," he wrote his wife from prison, "with both the time and the manner of my death, believing, as I now do, that for me at this time to seal my testimony for God and humanity with my blood will do vastly more toward advancing the cause I have earnestly endeavored to promote, than all I have done in my life before." So in his trial and in his last days in jail, Brown appeared the very picture of innocence: he insisted that he had never intended to provoke an insurrection (he also denied having anything whatever to do with the Pottawatomie killings). He had planned, he told the Charleston court, only a localized operation to liberate slaves and run them off to the North.

Brown was not telling the truth about his objectives, but in his mind what did it matter? In his exalted state, with an eye on the martyrdom that was nearly his now, he could easily rationalize all the erroneous and contradictory statements he gave about his purposes. For whatever he said to further the cause of liberty was not only right, it was the will of God.

As I have tried to demonstrate elsewhere in this book, Brown was a complicated and contradictory man—honest, deceitful, generous, dogmatic, affectionate, and egotistical by turns. There was a mesmerizing quality about him—a sense of moral rightness and a passionate concern for the exploited and oppressed—that earned him the respect of all kinds of people, from Kansas dirt farmers to Boston ministers and Concord transcendentalists. Yet there was such rage in him, such disillusionment and anger at his "slave-cursed" country, that he contemplated destroying it all.

Clearly the flawed, complex man who emerges from the historical record poses a sharp contrast to the godlike warrior who inhabits the writings of Truman Nelson. Of course, Nelson maintains that only his interpretation accords with the facts—that only he has "studied Brown right." But, in spite of such claims, I do not think that Nelson is really interested in the historical Brown. What he is concerned with is inflating Brown into "one of the great revolutionary figures of the ages," a hero's hero "as literal, tough-minded, and anarchic as nature itself." And woe indeed to anybody who disagrees with that. Woe to anybody who even suggests that Brown might have had an unfavorable trait or two, because in Nelson's doctrinaire mind (as is true of doctrinaires across the political spectrum) the world is a struggle between *right* and *wrong*. And John Brown was *right*. Anybody who ventures into the nuances between extremes, anybody who portrays Brown as a real-life human being who could love and hate, who had good and bad qualities, is an enemy of the revolution and deserves the ax.

All this is not to say that Brown has no meaning for our time. On the contrary, we can learn a great deal from Brown, if we avoid glorifying him and try to understand the man in the context of his own generation. We can learn why, out of the whirlpool of his own agonies and aspirations, John Brown became a revolutionary—why he rejected peaceful alternatives in favor of violent means (that most archetypical of American solutions) to remove injustice. And we can learn something about the society that produced him, too. For the United States of his day had institutionalized a monstrous moral contradiction: the existence of slavery in a Republic that claimed to be both Christian and free, a Republic founded on the enlightened ideal that everybody is entitled to life, liberty, and the pursuit of happiness. Unable (or unwilling) to resolve such a contradiction, the United States invited a messianic rebel like Brown to appear.

This, I contend, is how we should present John Brown to our students and our children—with an open mind, a scrupulous commitment to historical truth, an unshakable determination to examine all sides of Brown and all aspects of the flawed, racially troubled America in which he lived. Then, as with Nat Turner, perhaps we can perceive again the terrible cost of moral hypocrisy and retributive violence—of the continual failure of people to live with one another in a spirit of mutual tolerance and respect. But we can learn nothing, nothing at all, when modern advocates strip Brown of his historical realities and employ him to trumpet their own politics.

FIVE

THE ENIGMA OF STEPHEN A. DOUGLAS

E had all the traits of a prize fighter. More than anything else, he loved a good political brawl, the give and take of floor battles, and pugnacious oratory. In 1834, in Jacksonville, Illinois, he gave a roaring defense of Andrew Jackson, after which a cheering crowd swept him triumphantly out of the meetinghouse. From then on he was known as the Little Giant. Few had his capacity to intimidate, to outrage. John Quincy Adams was utterly astonished when the five-feet, four-inch Illinoisian, in one of his first speeches in the national House of Representatives, ripped off his cravat, unbuttoned his waistcoat, and with contorted face and wild gestures "lashed himself into such a heat that if his body had been made of combustible matter, it would have burnt out."

Stephen A. Douglas was a man of the political arena, an improviser and tough little pragmatist who never had the time or the inclination for deep reflection. From the age of twenty-one until he died, he sought political power with headlong impetuosity and unrelenting ambition. He always worked too hard, drank too much, and smoked too many cigars. Political defeat often left him sick and miserably depressed, but he drove himself on nevertheless. Above all, he was a man of contradiction and paradox. A nationalist who detested abolitionists and secessionists with equal passion, he was a confirmed party man, convinced that America was safe only in Democratic hands. By turns, he was an Anglophobe, a foe of the Know-Nothings, a defender of alien rights, and a friend of the Mormons. Like most white Americans of his generation, he thought Negroes repugnant and inferior. Yet he claimed that slavery was a curse on black and white alike. At the same time, he professed indifference as to whether slavery expanded or perished on these shores. Meanwhile, he owned a large Mississippi plantation and some 140 slaves. To ease sectional tensions, he tried to bypass the moral issue of slavery by espousing popular sovereignty, a principle that was deliberately ambiguous and ultimately unworkable. Naive, abusive, contradictory, practical, and visionary all at the same time, Douglas believed passionately in the United States, in her manifest destiny to rule this continent and to expand her commercial empire.

For fifteen years, the Little Giant was in the thick of some of America's most crucial political struggles. During the secession crisis, he searched about desperately for some compromise that might hold the Union together, and finally surrendered his own version of popular sovereignty in supporting the Crittenden resolutions. After Sumter, though, he demanded a strong war policy. Just when he might have become undisputed leader of a loyal opposition party, he died of "acute rheumatism" at the age of forty-eight. His life was so frenetic, his career so stormy and inconsistent, his eclipse so rapid, that ever since writers have had a difficult time explaining and assessing him.

If historians like James Ford Rhodes saw Douglas as an unscrupulous demagogue, a procession of biographies—from James W. Sheahan's 1860 campaign document down to Gerald Caper's *Stephen A. Douglas, Defender of the Union* (1959)—eulogized the Little Giant as one of America's most powerful and farsighted statesmen. The most complete deification appeared in George Fort Milton's *The Eve of Conflict: Stephen A. Douglas and the Needless War* (1934), a work that belonged to the so-called revisionist school of Civil War historiography. In Milton's view, the Little Giant was an immortal hero in an ignoble era: an eloquent champion of popular government assailed on all sides by scheming congressmen—Republicans and Southerners alike—and dimwitted presidents. Douglas introduced the Kansas-Nebraska bill, not because he wanted Southern support in his drive for the presidency (which was Rhodes's interpretation), but because he was a spokesman for western expansion and a Pacific railroad. The West had to be settled, Milton argued, and organizing Kansas and Nebraska was merely part of America's westering process. Nor was popular sovereignty a proslavery measure. In adopting it, Douglas tried to solve the problem of slavery in the territories by applying the principle of local self-government—that is, by letting the people of each territory decide whether to have bondage or not. "A realist in an emotional age," Douglas almost singlehandedly held the nation together from warring extremists in both sections—from abolitionist radicals in the North and blood-and-thunder disunionists in the South. And when "the needless war" came, a war Douglas had struggled with all his might to avoid, the Little Giant gave himself proudly to the Union cause and died (in the words of Alexander H. Stephens) "the foremost politician and statesman of his time."

In more recent years, with the renewed interest in slavery as a real and fundamental issue in the sectional controversy, historians have been a good deal more critical of Douglas. Allan Nevins, for his part, portrayed him as a flawed party leader—now courageous, now abysmally misguided. And in volume 2 of *The Ordeal of the Union* (1947), Nevins particularly chastized Douglas for the Kansas-Nebraska Act.* It was a monumental fiasco, one that split the Democratic party, delivered the coup de grace to the Whigs, enraged Northern free-soilers (which cost Douglas the Democratic presidential nomination in 1856), cleared the way for the appearance of a powerful new sectional party, and brought civil war a long step closer. Why was Douglas seemingly oblivious to the strength of Northern free-soil opinion? Because, Nevins contended, the Little Giant did not himself have a genuine dislike of slavery —did not care whether that institution was voted up or down— and erroneously believed that most Northerners felt as he did. Though Douglas sponsored the Nebraska bill for a variety of reasons, Nevins suggested that the man's driving impetuosity, his penchant for improvisation, may account for the repeal of the Missouri Compromise line. In the heat of the Nebraska struggle, he embraced popular sovereignty as an expedient to stop the slavery agitation; and once he had committed himself, once the free-soilers assailed him, he plunged forward like a maddened bull, knowing all the while that popular sovereignty had no historical precedent or constitutional justification. Yet in his fight against Buchanan and the Lecompton Constitution, which Nevins recounted in volume 1 of *The Emergence of Lincoln* (1950), Douglas

---

* There is a full discussion of the Kansas-Nebraska Act in the next chapter.

became "a great American leader," perhaps not so great as Lincoln, who rightly understood that a moral crisis over slavery had to be met and passed, but a gallant American nonetheless.

Other recent historians have also challenged Milton's interpretation, further tarnishing Douglas's image as the greatest statesman of his time. Harry Jaffa, in *Crisis of the House Divided* (1959), analyzed the rival positions of Douglas and Lincoln and concluded that the latter was right: slavery was a real and profound issue which could not be ignored. Unlike Nevins, Jaffa insisted that Douglas had an honest disdain for slavery, but could not commit himself publicly because it would have destroyed the Democratic party had he done so. Nor was Douglas evading the issue, for he was convinced that popular sovereignty would bring about a free-soil victory in the West. Forced against his better judgment to repeal the Missouri Compromise line, he attempted to squelch the slavery controversy with an appeal to patriotism and manifest destiny. Yet "at a moment when national purposes were confused and national identity obscured, patriotism was not enough," Jaffa wrote. And so it was Lincoln who, in making "morally certain" that the federal government maintained "national political responsibility," emerged as the greater man.

Douglas fared little better in Damon Wells's *Stephen Douglas, the Last Years* (1971), an often perceptive work, particularly in the chapter on popular sovereignty. Because Douglas championed that dubious principle as well as an outmoded concept of nationalism, Wells concluded that the Little Giant was tragically out-of-step with his times. Yet after war broke out Douglas abandoned his old posturings and became a devout Unionist, a role in which "he found his true greatness."

And now we have Robert W. Johannsen's long-awaited *Stephen A. Douglas* (1973), an encyclopedic work based on massive research in both published and unpublished sources. Plainly Johannsen has attempted a synthesis, drawing not only on his own findings and analysis, but on the views of Milton, Nevins, Jaffa, and many others, to produce just about the most detailed portrait of the Little Giant that we shall ever need. Johannsen's Douglas is a flawed hero, an often misunderstood, yet paradoxical man who could be visionary as well as myopic, noble as well as repelling. While Johannsen is sympathetic with his subject, he presents Douglas's least desirable traits (his racism, for instance) as scrupulously as he documents the Little Giant's achievements.

His first notable success came in Illinois, where in the 1830s and 1840s he built an inchoate Democratic party into a powerful and cohesive machine and became its "generalissimo." In his party work, Douglas proved himself both a skilled organizer and a man of principle, committed to the idea of popular self-government. Only through a well-defined political party, Douglas believed, could the popular will be adequately expressed.

During the 1840s, first in the national House and then in the Senate (where he became chairman of the powerful committee on territories), Douglas gradually worked out what Johannsen terms his western program. It called for territorial acquisition and organization, intensive railroad construction (with lines running from Illinois out to the Pacific and into the South), homestead legislation, and river and harbor improvements. Douglas's overriding commitment to this program, Johannsen insists, best accounts for the Little Giant's controversial "solutions" to slavery in the territories. Throughout the Mexican War and the debates over the Wilmot Proviso, Douglas's central purpose was to organize the West, including the new lands acquired from Mexico, as rapidly and efficiently as possible. But the fight over slavery kept getting in his way. So, being a hard-nosed pragmatist, he looked for expedients that would stop the controversy so he could get on with his work. First he advocated that the Missouri Compromise line be extended to the Pacific—a move, however, that Northern free-soilers blocked. Gradually, from 1848 to 1850, Douglas embraced popular sovereignty as the answer he was looking for—as a useful device that would banish the accursed slavery problem to the frontier. Then the federal government could concentrate on things Douglas thought were more important, such as enacting his western program, buying Cuba, and driving the British out of this hemisphere.

When he proposed popular sovereignty during the 1850 debates, Northern free-soilers castigated him as a "dough-face" out to extend slave territory. On this point, Johannsen defends Douglas as Jaffa and others have done, contending that in reality the Little Giant was himself a free-soiler. According to Johannsen, Douglas announced again and again that popular sovereignty was an antislavery measure, that under its banners both freedom and Northern enterprises would triumph in the West.

Then came the explosive Kansas-Nebraska Act. Johannsen, revising both Jaffa and Roy F. Nichols, persuasively demonstrates that Douglas was almost solely responsible for the initial 1854 bill and the subsequent alterations, including the explicit repeal of the Missouri Compromise line.* Why did the senator obliterate a measure he had once voted to extend? Because he now believed the Missouri line a nuisance that kept the slavery question ablaze in Congress. So away with the line altogether. What Douglas wanted was a panacea that would solve his and the nation's woes —a cure-all that would permanently silence the slavery controversy, so that the United States could get on with its empire building, and that would also unite a badly split Democratic party. And popular sovereignty, Douglas decided, was that panacea. So, with the help of several powerful Southern politicians, he rammed the Kansas-Nebraska bill through a divided Congress. The final version of the enactment declared the Missouri line "inoperative," advancing the utterly fallacious argument that the Compromise of 1850 had "superceded" that of 1820 and had established popular sovereignty as the new formula for dealing with slavery in the territories. Douglas, for his part, was now driven to defend popular sovereignty as "a sacred principle," elevating to the lofty heights of a "higher law" what he had initially seized as merely a useful expedient. By applying the cherished principle of self-government and relegating the slavery question to the territories, Douglas hoped that somehow everything would turn out all right.

But everything did not turn out all right, for popular sovereignty contained a fatal ambiguity that inflamed the slave controversy worse than ever. At what point could the people of a territory sustain or prohibit slavery? If Southerners maintained that this could be done only at the time of statehood, Douglas vaguely insisted that the institution could be dealt with at any territorial stage. Precisely because the doctrine was ambiguous, because it was open to the kind of interpretation Douglas gave it, Southern-

---

* Nichols, in "The Kansas-Nebraska Act: A Century of Historiography," *Mississippi Valley Historical Review* 43 (September 1956), 187–212, held that it was not Douglas who brought about the final version of that enactment or the repeal of the Missouri Compromise that it contained; rather, these grow out of a complex process of political maneuvering and power struggles within the Democratic party.

ers never really embraced popular sovereignty. Soon they were attacking it as a sinister free-soil device. At the same time, Northern free-soilers denounced it as part of a Slave-Power conspiracy. Douglas fought back savagely—especially against the Southerners. The latter's suspicions about him seemed confirmed when the senator challenged the proslavery Lecompton Constitution—the fruit of his own unhappy program—drawn up in the Kansas Territory. Then came Douglas's so-called Freeport doctrine: that settlers could effectively prohibit slavery before statehood by refusing to pass the police measures necessary to sustain it. Actually Douglas had propounded the doctrine of "unfriendly legislation" several times before. But reiterating it at Freeport, in all the excitement of the Lincoln-Douglas debates of 1858, created a sensation. As a consequence of Freeport, says Johannsen, Southern leaders felt obliged to demand a congressional slave code in the territories, regarding this as the only weapon that could counter Douglas's doctrine of unfriendly legislation. Of course the champion of popular sovereignty, with its corollary of absolute congressional nonintervention, could never accept such a code. As a result, Douglas and Southern leaders were locked in their own irrepressible conflict which ultimately split their party.

By now Douglas was trapped in a terrible paradox: he was trying to hold the nation and the Democrats together with a principle that was helping to tear them both apart. To make matters worse, the senator did not always adhere to his own cherished principles of nonintervention and local self-government. In 1857, when word came of the Mormon troubles in Utah, Douglas implored the president to send troops there and even suggested that Congress ought to rescind Utah's territorial status. Moreover, his erratic behavior in the crucial 1860 election only added to the storm of confusion that surrounded the man. As he stumped the South, he announced that he was no longer running for the presidency, but was trying only to prevent secession and save the Union. Yet he refused to withdraw in favor of a candidate more acceptable to the South, refused to participate in any of the various fusion movements, because he was the only man, he declared, who could defeat Lincoln (even though the senator regarded a Lincoln victory as just about inevitable). Meanwhile, in the North, South, and West the Little Giant continued to trumpet the virtues of popular sovereignty. It says something about the times that, when all the ballots were in, this vague, blusterous, inconsistent man was second only to Lincoln in popular votes.

In the ensuing secession crisis, Johannsen like George Fort Milton inflates the Little Giant into an immortal American hero. Here again is the olympian statesman, trying almost singlehandedly to forge a compromise between Republicans and Southerners that would save his country. But, Johannsen writes, he is blocked by "a united phalanx of Republican Senators," who, for partisan reasons, vote down one compromise measure after another. Johannsen implies that Lincoln and his Republican colleagues were largely responsible for the failure of conciliation and the onset of Civil War. And that is unfair. After all, for the Republicans to compromise over slavery in the territories—which was what the measures called for—would be to surrender their program of slave containment, the raison d'etre of their party. "Let there be no compromise on the question of *extending* slavery," Lincoln ordered his colleagues. Once concessions are made, "immediately filibustering and extending slavery recommences" and "leaves all our work to do over again." Furthermore, Douglas and the Northern and border-state Democrats were just as intractable, refusing to accept the platform on which Lincoln had been fairly and legally elected and clinging tenaciously to proposals that would allow slavery to expand. And in any case, what did the seceded states care about the compromise plans introduced in Washington? Those states were gone, out of the Union, building a new slave-based nation in Dixie, and no amount of promises and guarantees was going to bring them back.

So, in spite of Douglas's conciliatory efforts, the Civil War came. In the closing scenes of Johannsen's book, we find Douglas calling at Lincoln's office and offering the president his undivided support. The Little Giant "cordially" approves of Lincoln's call for 75,000 troops to suppress the rebels, except that "I would make it 200,000," Douglas says. "You do not know the dishonest purposes of those men as well as I do." Then we see him hurrying home to rally conservative Democrats to the Union banner (and to build a political power base for himself), only to die his premature death, having "consecrated his life to the cause, and staked his fortunes on the result."

Johannsen's volume contains a wealth of information about these and virtually all other aspects of Douglas's life (his two marriages, his real-estate speculations, his law practice), rendering this an indispensable reference work. But I question whether it is really biography. In his determination to get in all the facts, Johannsen often loses sight of his subject, burying Douglas himself in a cascade of details about such background events as the outbreak of the Mexican War, the organization of the Republican party in Illinois, and the complex maneuverings at Charleston and Baltimore in 1860. In my judgment, the book would be far more successful as biography—and still a formidable scholarly achievement—had the author trimmed away about 200 of the 874 pages of text.

Moreover, not everyone will share Johannsen's sympathies for the Little Giant. Though the author is at pains to vindicate Douglas as a free-soiler with a greater vision of expansion and empire, one can appreciate why legitimate free-soilers questioned the senator's antislavery credentials. After all, the man was a slaveowner. Furthermore, by Johannsen's own account, the Little Giant lovingly tended the Mississippi plantation, whose profits helped sustain him in politics so that he could defend popular sovereignty. But this was characteristic of a strangely imperceptive man who, down to the very end, was ensnared in his own ambiguities and contradictions.

SIX

LINCOLN'S JOURNEY TO EMANCIPATION

I

H E comes to us in the mists of legend as a kind of homespun Socrates, brimming with prairie wit and folk wisdom. He is as honest, upright, God-fearing, generous, and patriotic an American as the Almighty ever created. Impervious to material rewards and social station, the Lincoln of mythology is the Great Commoner, a saintly Rail Splitter who spoke in a deep, fatherly voice about the genius of the plain folk. He comes to us, too, as the Great Emancipator who led the North off to Civil War to free the slaves and afterward offered his fellow Southerners a tender and forgiving hand.

There is a counterlegend of Lincoln—one shared ironically enough by many white Southerners and certain black Americans of our time. This is the legend of Lincoln as bigot, as a white racist who championed segregation, opposed civil and political rights for black people, wanted them all thrown out of the country. This Lincoln is the great ancestor of racist James K. Vardaman of Mississippi, of "Bull" Connor of Birmingham, of the white citizens' councils, of the Knights of the Ku Klux Klan.

Neither of these views, of course, reveals much about the man who really lived—legends and politicized interpretations seldom do. The real Lincoln was not a saintly emancipator, and he was not an unswerving racist either. To understand him and the liberation of the slaves, one must eschew artificial, arbitrary categories and focus on the man as he lived, on the flesh-and-blood Lincoln, on that flawed and fatalistic individual who struggled with himself and his countrymen over the profound moral paradox of slavery in a nation based on the Declaration of Independence. Only by viewing Lincoln scrupulously in the context of his own time can one understand the painful, ironic, and troubled journey that led him to the Emancipation Proclamation and to the Thirteenth Amendment that made it permanent.

II

As a man, Lincoln was complex, many-sided, and richly human. He was almost entirely self-educated, with a talent for expression that in another time and place might have led him into a literary career. He wrote poetry himself and studied Shakespeare, Byron, and Oliver Wendell Holmes, attracted especially to writings with tragic and melancholy themes. He examined the way celebrated orators turned a phrase or employed a figure of speech, admiring great truths greatly told. Though never much at impromptu oratory, he could hold an audience of 15,000 spellbound when reading from a written speech, singing out in a shrill, high-pitched voice that became his trademark.

He was an intense, brooding person, plagued with chronic depression most of his life. "I am now the most miserable man living," he said on one occasion in 1841. "If what I feel were equally distributed to the whole human family, there would not be one cheerful face on the earth." He added, "To remain as I am is impossible; I must die or be better."

At the time he said this, Lincoln had fears of sexual inadequacy, doubting his ability to please or even care for a wife. In 1842 he confided in his closest friend, Joshua Speed, about his troubles, and both confessed that they had fears of "nervous debility" with women. Speed went ahead and married anyway and then wrote Lincoln that their anxieties were groundless. "I tell you, Speed, our forebodings, for which you and I are rather peculiar, are all the worst sort of nonsense," Lincoln rejoiced. Encouraged by Speed's success, Lincoln finally wedded Mary Todd; and she obviously helped him overcome his doubts, for they developed a strong and lasting physical love for one another.

Still, Lincoln remained a moody, melancholy man, given to long introspections about things like death and mortality. In truth, death was a lifelong obsession with him. His poetry, speeches, and letters are studded with allusions to it. He spoke of the transitory nature of human life, spoke of how all people in this world are fated to die in the end—all are fated to die. He saw himself as only a passing moment in a rushing river of time.

Preoccupied with death, he was also afraid of insanity, afraid (as he phrased it) of "the pangs that kill the mind." In his late thirties, he wrote and rewrote a poem about a boyhood friend, one Matthew Gentry, who became deranged and was locked "in mental night," condemned to a living death, spinning out of control in some inner void. Lincoln retained a morbid fascination with Gentry's condition, writing about how Gentry was more an object of dread than death itself: "A human form with reason fled, while wretched life remains." Yet, Lincoln was fascinated with madness, troubled by it, afraid that what had happened to Matthew could also happen to him—his own reason destroyed, Lincoln spinning in mindless night without the power to know.

Lincoln was a teetotaler because liquor left him "flabby and undone," blurring his mind and threatening his self-control. And he dreaded and avoided anything which threatened that. In one memorable speech, he heralded some great and distant day when all passions would be subdued, when reason would triumph and "*mind, all conquering mind*," would rule the earth.

One side of Lincoln was always supremely logical and analytical. He was intrigued with the clarity of mathematics; and as an attorney he could command a mass of technical data. Yet he was also extremely superstitious, believed in signs and visions, contended that dreams were auguries of approaching triumph or calamity. He was skeptical of organized religion and never joined a church; yet he argued that all human destinies were controlled by an omnipotent God.

It is true that Lincoln told folksy anecdotes to illustrate a point. But humor was also tremendous therapy for his depressions—a device "to whistle down sadness," as a friend put it. Lincoln liked all kinds of jokes, from bawdy tales to pungent rib-ticklers like "Bass-Ackwards," a story he wrote down and handed a bailiff one day. Filled with hilarious spoonerisms, "Bass-Ackwards" is about a fellow who gets thrown from his horse and lands in "a great tow-curd," which gives him a "*sick* of *fitness*." About "*bray dake*," he comes to and dashes home to find "the *door* sick abed, and his *wife* standing open. But thank goodness," the punch line goes, "she is getting right *hat* and *farty* again."

Contrary to legend, Lincoln was anything but a common man. In point of fact, he was one of the most ambitious human beings his friends had ever seen, with an aspiration for high station in life that burned in him like a furnace. Instead of reading with an accomplished attorney, as was customary in those days, he taught himself the law entirely on his own. He was literally a self-made lawyer. Moreover, he entered the Illinois legislature at the age of twenty-five and became a leader of the state Whig party, a tireless party campaigner, and a regular candidate for public office.

As a self-made man, Lincoln felt embarrassed about his log-cabin origins and never liked to talk about them. He seldom discussed his parents either and became permanently estranged from his father, who was all but illiterate. In truth, Lincoln had considerable hostility for his father's intellectual limitations, once remarking that Thomas "never did more in the way of writing than to bunglingly sign his own name." When his father died in a nearby Illinois county in 1851, Lincoln did not attend the funeral.

By the 1850s, Lincoln was one of the most sought-after attorneys in Illinois, with a reputation as a lawyer's lawyer—a knowledgeable jurist who argued appeal cases for other attorneys. He did his most influential legal work in the Supreme Court of Illinois, where he participated in 243 cases and won most of them. He commanded the respect of his colleagues, all of whom called him "Mr. Lincoln" or just "Lincoln." Nobody called him Abe—at least not to his face—because he loathed the nickname. It did not befit a respected professional who'd struggled hard to overcome the limitations of his frontier background. Frankly Lincoln enjoyed his status as a lawyer and politician, and he liked money, too, and used it to measure his worth. By the mid-1850s, thanks to a combination of talent and sheer hard work, Lincoln was a man of substantial wealth. He had an annual income of around $5,000— the equivalent of many times that today—and large financial and real-estate investments.

Though a man of status and influence, Lincoln was as honest in real life as in the legend. Even his enemies conceded that he was incorruptible. Moreover, he possessed broad humanitarian views, some of them in advance of his time. Even though he was a teetotaler, he was extremely tolerant of alcoholics, regarding them not as criminals—the way most temperance people did—but as unfortunates who deserved understanding, not vilification. He noted that some of the world's most gifted artists had succumbed to alcoholism, because they were too sensitive to cope with their insights into the human condition. He believed that women, like men, should vote so long as they all paid taxes. And he had no ethnic prejudices. His law partner William Herndon, who cursed the Irish with a flourish, reported that Lincoln was not at all prejudiced against "the foreign element, tolerating—as I never could—even the Irish."

Politically, Lincoln was always a nationalist in outlook, an outlook that began when he was an Indiana farm boy tilling his father's mundane wheat field. While the plow horse was getting its breath at the end of a furrow, Lincoln would study Parson Weems's eulogistic biography of George Washington, and he would daydream about the Revolution and the origins of the Republic, daydream about Washington and Jefferson as great national statesmen who shaped the course of history. By the time he became a politician, Lincoln idolized the Founding Fathers as apostles of liberty (never mind for now that many of these apostles were also Southern slaveowners). Young Lincoln extolled the founders for beginning an experiment in popular government on this continent, to show a doubting Europe that people could govern themselves without hereditary monarchs and aristocracies. And the foundation of the American experiment was the Declaration of Independence, which in Lincoln's view contained the highest political truths in history: that all men are created equal and are entitled to freedom and the pursuit of happiness. Which for Lincoln meant that men like him were not chained to the condition of their births, that they could better their station in life and harvest the fruits of their own talents and industry. Thus he had a deep, personal reverence for the Declaration and insisted that all his political sentiments flowed from that document.

III

Which brings us to the problem and paradox of slavery in America. Lincoln maintained that he had always hated human bondage, as much as any abolitionist. His family had opposed the peculiar institution, and Lincoln had grown up and entered Illinois politics thinking it wrong. But before 1854 (and the significance of that date will become clear) Lincoln generally kept his own counsel about slavery and abolition. After all, slavery was the most inflammable issue of his generation, and Lincoln observed early on what violent passions Negro bondage—and the question of race that underlay it—could arouse in white Americans. In his day, as I have said, slavery was a tried and tested means of race control in a South absolutely dedicated to white supremacy. Moreover, the North was also a white supremacist region, where the vast majority of whites opposed emancipation lest it result in a flood of Southern blacks into the free states. And Illinois was no exception, as most whites there were against abolition and were anti-Negro to the core. Lincoln, who had elected to work within the system, was not going to ruin his career by espousing an extremely unpopular cause. To be branded as an abolitionist in central Illinois—his constituency as a legislator and a U.S. congressman—would have been certain political suicide. At the same time, attorney Lincoln conceded that Southern slavery had become a thoroughly entrenched institution, that bondage where it already existed was protected by the Constitution and could not be molested by the national government.

Still, slavery distressed him. He realized how wrong it was that slavery should exist at all in a self-proclaimed free and enlightened Republic. He who cherished the Declaration of Independence understood only too well how bondage mocked and contradicted that noble document. Too, he thought slavery a blight on the American experiment in popular government. It was, he believed, the one retrograde institution that robbed the Republic of its just example in the world, robbed the United States of the hope it should hold out to oppressed people everywhere.

He opposed slavery, too, because he had witnessed some of its evils firsthand. In 1841, on a steamboat journey down the Ohio River, he saw a group of manacled slaves on their way to the cruel cotton plantations of the Deep South. Lincoln was appalled at the sight of those chained Negroes. Fourteen years later he wrote that the spectacle "was a continual torment to me" and that he saw something like it every time he touched a slave border. Slavery, he said, "had the power of making me miserable."

Again, while serving in Congress from 1847 to 1849, he passed slave auction blocks in Washington, D.C. In fact, from the windows of the Capitol, he could observe the infamous "Georgia pen" —"a sort of Negro livery stable," as he described it, "where droves of negroes were collected, temporarily kept, and finally taken to Southern markets, precisely like droves of horses." The spectacle offended him. He agreed with a Whig colleague that the buying and selling of human beings in the United States capital was a national disgrace. Accordingly Lincoln drafted a gradual abolition bill for the District of Columbia. But powerful Southern politicians howled in protest, and his own Whig support fell away. At that, Lincoln dropped his bill and sat in glum silence as Congress rocked with debates—with drunken fights and rumbles of disunion— over the status of slavery out in the territories. Shocked at the behavior of his colleagues, Lincoln confessed that slavery was the one issue that threatened the stability of the Union.

What could be done? Slavery as an institution could not be removed, and yet it should not remain either. Trapped in what seemed an impossible dilemma, Lincoln persuaded himself that if slavery were confined to the South and left alone there, time would somehow solve the problem and slavery would ultimately die out. And he told himself that the Founding Fathers had felt the same way, that they too had expected slavery to perish some day. In Lincoln's interpretation, they had tolerated slavery as a necessary evil, agreeing that it could not be eradicated where it already flourished without causing wide-scale wreckage. But in his view they had taken steps to restrict its growth (had excluded slavery from the old Northwest territories, had outlawed the international slave trade) and so had placed the institution on the road to extinction.

So went Lincoln's argument before 1854. The solution was to bide one's time, trust the future to get rid of slavery and square America with her own ideals. And he convinced himself that when slavery was no longer workable, Southern whites would gradually liberate the blacks on their own. They would do so voluntarily.

To solve the ensuing problem of racial adjustment, Lincoln insisted that the federal government should colonize all blacks in Africa, an idea he got from his political idol, Whig national leader Henry Clay. Said Lincoln in 1852: if the Republic could remove the danger of slavery and restore "a captive people to their long-lost father-land," and do both so gradually "that neither races nor individuals shall have suffered by the change," then "it will indeed be a glorious consummation."

IV

Then came 1854 and the momentous Kansas-Nebraska Act, brainchild of Lincoln's archrival Stephen A. Douglas. The act overturned the old Missouri Compromise line, which excluded slavery from the vast northern area of the old Louisiana Purchase territory. The act then established a new formula for dealing with slavery in the national lands: now Congress would stay out of the matter, and the people of each territory would decide whether to retain or outlaw the institution. Until such time as the citizens of a territory voted on the issue, Southerners were free to take slavery into most western territories, including the new ones of Kansas and Nebraska. These were carved out of the northern section of the old Louisiana Purchase territory. Thanks to the Kansas-Nebraska Act, a northern domain once preserved for freedom now seemed open to a proslavery invasion.

At once a storm of free-soil protest broke across the North, and scores of political leaders branded the Kansas-Nebraska Act as part of a sinister Southern plot to extend slave territory and augment Southern political power in Washington. There followed a series of political upheavals. A civil war blazed up in Kansas, as proslavery and free-soil pioneers came into bloody collisions on the prairie there—proof that slavery was far too volatile ever to be solved as a purely local matter. At the same time, the old Whig party disintegrated. In its place emerged the all-Northern Republican party, dedicated to blocking slavery extension and to saving the cherished frontier for free white labor. Then in 1857 came the infamous Dred Scott decision, handed down by Taney's pro-Southern Supreme Court, which ruled that neither Congress nor a territorial government could outlaw slavery, because that would violate Southern property rights. As Lincoln and many others observed, the net effect of the decision was to legalize slavery in all federal territories from Canada to Mexico.

The train of ominous events from Kansas-Nebraska to Dred Scott shook Lincoln to his foundations. In his view, the Southern-controlled Democratic party—the party that dominated the Senate, the Supreme Court, and the presidency—had instituted a revolt against the Founding Fathers and the entire course of the Republic so far as slavery was concerned. Now human bondage was not going to die out. Now it was going to expand and grow and continue indefinitely, as Southerners dragged manacled Negroes across the West, adapting slave labor to whatever conditions they found there, putting the blacks to work in mines and on farms. Now Southerners would create new slave states in the West and make slavery powerful and permanent in America. Now the Republic would never remove the cancer that infected its political system, would never remove the one institution that marred its global image, would never remove a "cruel wrong" that mocked the Declaration of Independence.

Lincoln waded into the middle of the antiextension fight. He campaigned for the national Senate. He joined the Republican party. He thundered against the evil designs of the "Slave Power." He spoke with an urgent sense of mission that gave his speeches a searching eloquence—a mission to save the Republic's noblest ideals, turn back the tide of slavery expansion, restrict the peculiar institution once again to the South, and place it back on the road to extinction, as Lincoln believed the Founding Fathers had so placed it.

By 1858, Lincoln, like a lot of other Republicans, began to see a grim proslavery conspiracy at work in the United States. The first stage was to betray the founders and send slavery flooding all over the West. At the same time, proslavery theorists were out to undermine the Declaration of Independence, to discredit its equality doctrine as "a self-evident lie" (as many Southern spokesmen were actually saying), and to replace the Declaration with the principles of inequality and human servitude.

The next step in the conspiracy would be to nationalize slavery: the Taney Court, Lincoln feared, would hand down another decision, one declaring that states could not prohibit slavery either. Then the institution would sweep into Illinois, sweep into Indiana and Ohio, sweep into Pennsylvania and New York, sweep into Massachusetts and New England, sweep all over the Northern states, until at last slavery would be nationalized and America would end up a slave house. At that, as George Fitzhugh advocated, the conspirators would enslave all American workers regardless of color. The Northern free-labor system would be expunged, the Declaration of Independence overthrown, self-government abolished, and the conspirators would restore despotism with class rule and an entrenched aristocracy. All the work since the Revolution of 1776 would be obliterated. The world's best hope—America's experiment in popular government—would be destroyed, and mankind would spin backward into feudalism.

For Lincoln and his Republican colleagues, it was imperative that the conspiracy be blocked in its initial stage—the expansion of slavery into the West. In 1858 Lincoln set out after Douglas's Senate seat, inveighing against the Little Giant for his part in the proslavery plot and warning Illinois—and Northerners beyond—that only the Republicans could save their free-labor system and their free government. Now Lincoln openly and fiercely declaimed his antislavery sentiments. He hated the institution. He hated slavery because it degraded blacks and whites alike. Because it prevented the Negro from "eating the bread which his own hand earns." Because it not only contradicted the Declaration, but violated the principles of free labor, self-help, social mobility, and economic independence, all of which lay at the center of Republican ideology, of Lincoln's ideology. Yet, while branding slavery as an evil and doing all they could to contain it in the South, Republicans would not, could not, molest the institution in those states where it already existed.

Douglas, fighting for his political life in free-soil Illinois, lashed back at Lincoln with unadulterated race-baiting. Throughout the Great Debates of 1858, Douglas smeared Lincoln and his party as Black Republicans, as a gang of radical abolitionists out to liberate all Southern slaves and bring them stampeding into Illinois and the rest of the North, where they would take away white jobs and copulate with white daughters. Again and again, Douglas accused Lincoln of desiring intermarriage and racial mongrelization.

Lincoln protested emphatically that race was not the issue between him and Douglas. The issue was whether slavery would ultimately triumph or ultimately perish in the United States. But Douglas understood the depth of anti-Negro feeling in Illinois, and he hoped to whip Lincoln by playing on white racial fears.

Forced to take a stand lest Douglas ruin him with his allegations, Lincoln conceded that he was not for Negro political or social equality. He was not for enfranchising Negroes, was not for intermarriage. There was, he said, "a physical difference" between blacks and whites that would "probably" always prevent them from living together in perfect equality. Having confessed his racial views, Lincoln then qualified them: if Negroes were not the equal of Lincoln and Douglas in moral or intellectual endowment, they *were* equal to Lincoln, Douglas, and "every living man" in their right to liberty, equality of opportunity, and the fruits of their own labor. (Later he insisted that it was bondage that had "clouded" the slaves' intellects and that Negroes were capable of thinking like whites.) Moreover, Lincoln rejected "the counterfeit argument" that just because he did not want a black woman for a slave, he necessarily wanted her for a wife. He could just let her alone. He could let her alone so that she could also enjoy her freedom and "her natural right to eat the bread she earns with her own hands."

Exasperated with Douglas and white Negrophobia in general, Lincoln begged American whites "to discard all this quibbling about this man and the other man—this race and that race and the other race as being inferior," begged them to unite as one people and defend the ideals of the Declaration and its promise of liberty and opportunity for all.

Lincoln lost the 1858 Senate contest to Douglas. But in 1860 he won the Republican nomination for president and stood before the American electorate on the free-soil, free-labor principles of the Republican party. As the Republican standard bearer, Lincoln was uncompromising in his determination to prohibit slavery in the territories by national law and to save the Republic (as he put it) from returning "class, caste, and despotism." He exhorted his fellow Republicans to stand firm in their duty: to brand slavery as an evil, contain it in the South, look to the future for slavery to die a gradual death, and promise colonization to solve the question of race. Some day, somehow, the American house must be free of slavery. That was the Republican vision, the distant horizon Lincoln saw.

Yet, for the benefit of Southerners, he repeated that he and his party would not harm slavery in the Southern states. The federal government had no constitutional authority in peace time to tamper with a state institution like slavery.

But Southerners refused to believe anything Lincoln said. In

Dixie, orators and editors alike castigated him as a black-hearted radical, a "sooty and scoundrelly" abolitionist who wanted to free the slaves at once and mix the races. In Southern eyes, Lincoln was another John Brown, a mobocrat, a Southern hater, a chimpanzee, a lunatic, the "biggest ass in the United States," the evil chief of the North's "Black Republican, free love, free Nigger" party, whose victory would ring the bells of doom for the white man's South. Even if Southerners had to drench the Union in blood, cried an Atlanta man, "the South, the loyal South, the Constitution South, would never submit to such humiliation and degradation as the inauguration of Abraham Lincoln."

After Lincoln's victory and the secession of the Deep South, Lincoln beseeched Southerners to understand the Republican position on slavery. In his Inaugural Address of 1861, he assured them once again that the federal government would not free the slaves in the South, that it had no legal right to do so. He even gave his blessings to the original Thirteenth Amendment, just passed by Congress, that would have guaranteed slavery in the Southern states for as long as whites there wanted it. Lincoln endorsed the amendment because he thought it consistent with Republican ideology. Ironically, Southern secession and the outbreak of war prevented that amendment from ever being ratified.

When the rebels opened fire on Fort Sumter, the nation plunged into civil war, a conflict that began as a ninety-day skirmish for both sides, but that swelled instead into a vast and terrible carnage with consequences beyond calculation for those swept up in its flames. Lincoln, falling into a depression that would plague him through his embattled presidency, remarked that the war was the supreme irony of his life: that he who sickened at the sight of blood, who abhorred stridency and physical violence, was caught in a national holocaust, a tornado of blood and wreckage with Lincoln himself whirling in its center.

v

At the outset of the war, Lincoln strove to be consistent with all that he and his party had said about slavery: his purpose in the struggle was strictly to save the Union; it was not to free the slaves. He would crush the rebellion with his armies and restore the national authority in the South with slavery intact. Then Lincoln and his party would resume and implement their policy of slave containment.

There were other reasons for Lincoln's hands-off policy about slavery. Four slave states—Delaware, Maryland, Kentucky, and Missouri—remained in the Union. Should he try to free the slaves, Lincoln feared it would send the crucial border spiraling into the Confederacy, something that would be catastrophic for the Union. A Confederate Maryland would create an impossible situation for Washington, D.C. And a Confederate Missouri and Kentucky would give the rebels potential bases from which to invade Illinois, Indiana, and Ohio. So Lincoln rejected emancipation in part to appease the loyal border.

He was also waging a bipartisan war effort, with Northern Democrats and Republicans alike enlisting in his armies to save the Union. Lincoln encouraged this because he insisted that it would take a united North to win the war. An emancipation policy, he feared, would alienate Northern Democrats, ignite a racial powder keg in the Northern states, and possibly cause a civil war in the rear. Then the Union really would be lost.

But the pressures and problems of civil war caused Lincoln to change his mind, caused him to abandon his hands-off policy and hurl an executive fist at slavery in the rebel states, thus making emancipation a Union war objective. The pressures operating on Lincoln were complex and merit careful discussion.

First, from the summer of 1861 on, several Republican senators —chief among them, Charles Sumner of Massachusetts, Ben Wade of Ohio, and Zachariah Chandler of Michigan—sequestered themselves with Lincoln and implored and badgered him to free the slaves.* Sumner, as Lincoln's personal friend and chief foreign policy adviser, was especially persistent. Before secession, of course, Sumner and his colleagues had all adhered to the Republican position on slavery in the South. But civil war had now removed their constitutional scruples about the peculiar institution. After all, they told Lincoln, the Southern people were in rebellion

---

* These "more advanced Republicans," as the *Detroit Post and Tribune* referred to Sumner and his associates, belonged to a powerful minority faction of the party inaccurately categorized as "radicals," a misnomer that has persisted through the years. For a discussion of this point, see my article, "The Slaves Freed," *American Heritage* (December 1980), 74–83.

against the national government; they could not resist that government and yet enjoy the protection of its laws. Now the senators argued that the national government could eradicate slavery by the War Power, and they wanted Lincoln to do it in his capacity as commander-in-chief. If he emancipated the slaves, it would maim and cripple the Confederacy and hasten an end to the rebellion.

Second, they pointed out that slavery had caused the war, was the reason why the Southern states had seceded, and was now the cornerstone of the Confederacy. It was absurd, the senators contended, to fight a war without removing the thing that had brought it about. Should the South return to the Union with slavery intact, as Lincoln desired, Southerners would just start another war over slavery, whenever they thought it threatened again, so that the present struggle would have accomplished nothing, nothing at all. If Lincoln really wanted to save the Union, he must tear slavery out root and branch and smash the South's planter class—that mischievous class the senators thought had masterminded secession and fomented war.

Sumner, in his role as foreign policy adviser, also linked emancipation to foreign policy. On several occasions in 1861 and 1862, Britain seemed on the verge of recognizing the Confederacy as an independent nation—a move that would be calamitous for the Union. As a member of the family of nations, the Confederacy could form alliances and seek mediation and perhaps armed intervention in the American conflict. But, Sumner argued, if Lincoln made the obliteration of slavery a Union war aim, Britain would balk at recognition and intervention. Why so? Because she was proud of her antislavery tradition, Sumner contended, and would refrain from helping the South protect human bondage from Lincoln's armies. And whatever powerful Britain did, the rest of Europe was sure to follow.

Also, as Sumner kept reminding everyone, emancipation would break the chains of several million oppressed human beings and right America at last with her own ideals. Lincoln could no longer wait for the future to remove slavery. He must do it. The war, monstrous and terrible though it was, had given Lincoln the opportunity to do it.

There was still another argument for emancipation, an argument advanced not just by Sumner and his colleagues, but by members of Lincoln's cabinet as well. In 1862, his armies suffered from manpower shortages on every front. Thanks to repeated Union military failures and to a growing war weariness across the North, volunteering had fallen off sharply; and Union generals bombarded Washington with shrill complaints, insisting that they faced an overwhelming Southern foe and must have reinforcements before they could win battles or even fight. While Union commanders often exaggerated rebel strength, Union forces *did* need reinforcements to carry out a successful offensive war. As Sumner reminded Lincoln, the slaves were an untapped reservoir of strength. "You need more men," Sumner said, "not only at the North, but at the South. You need the slaves." If Lincoln freed them, he could recruit black men into his armed forces, thus helping to solve his manpower woes.

Lincoln was sympathetic to the entire range of arguments Sumner and his associates rehearsed for him. Personally, Lincoln hated slavery as much as they did, and many of their points had already occurred to him. In fact, as early as November and December 1861, Lincoln began wavering in his hands-off policy about slavery, began searching about for some compromise—something short of a sweeping emancipation decree. Again he seemed caught in an impossible dilemma: how to remove the cause of the war, keep Britain out of the conflict, cripple the Confederacy and suppress the rebellion, and yet retain the allegiance of Northern Democrats and the critical border?

In March 1862, he proposed a plan to Congress he thought might work: a gradual, compensated emancipation program to commence in the loyal border states. According to Lincoln's plan, the border states would gradually abolish slavery themselves over the next thirty years, and the federal government would compensate slaveowners for their loss. The whole program was to be voluntary; the states would adopt their own emancipation laws without federal coercion.

At the same time, the federal government would sponsor a colonization program, which was also to be entirely voluntary. Without a promise of colonization, Lincoln understood only too well, most Northern whites would never accept emancipation, even if it were carried out by the states. From now on, every time he contemplated some new antislavery move, he made a great fuss about colonization: he embarked on a colonization project in central America and another in Haiti, and he held an interview about colonization with Washington's black leaders, an interview he published in the press. In part, the ritual of colonization was designed to calm white racial fears.

If his gradual, state-guided plan were adopted, Lincoln contended that a presidential decree—federally enforced emancipation—would never be necessary. Abolition would begin on the local level in the loyal border and then be extended into the rebel states as they were conquered. Thus by a slow and salubrious process would the cause of the rebellion be removed and the future of the Union guaranteed.

The plan failed. It failed because the border states refused to act. Lincoln couldn't even persuade Delaware, with its small and relatively harmless slave population, to adopt his program. In desperation, Lincoln on three different occasions—in the spring and summer of 1862—pleaded with border-state congressmen to endorse his program. In their third meeting, held in the White House on July 12, Lincoln warned the border representatives that it was impossible now to restore the Union with slavery preserved. Slavery was doomed. They could not be blind to the signs, blind to the fact that his plan was the only alternative to a more drastic move against slavery, one that would cause tremendous destruction in the South. Please, he said, commend my gradual plan to your people.

But most of the border men turned him down. They thought his plan would cost too much, would only whip the flames of rebellion, would cause dangerous discontent in their own states. Their intransigence was a sober lesson to Lincoln. It was proof indeed that slaveowners—even loyal slaveowners—were too tied up in the slave system ever to free their own Negroes and voluntarily transform their way of life. If abolition must come, it must begin in the rebel South and then be extended into the loyal border later on. Which meant that the president must eradicate slavery himself. He could no longer avoid the responsibility. By mid-July 1862, the pressures of the war had forced him to abandon his hands-off policy and lay a "strong hand on the colored element."

On July 13, the day after his last talk with the border men, Lincoln took a carriage ride with a couple of his cabinet secretaries. His conversation, when recounted in full, reveals a tougher Lincoln than the lenient and compromising president of the legend-building biographies. Lincoln said he was convinced that the war could no longer be won through forbearance toward Southern rebels, that it was "a duty on our part to liberate the slaves." The time had come to take a bold new path and hurl Union armies at "the heart of the rebellion," using the military to destroy the very institution that caused and now sustained the insurrection. Southerners could not throw off the Constitution and at the same time invoke it to protect slavery. They had started the war and must now face its consequences.

He had given this a lot of grave and painful thought, he said, and had concluded that a presidential declaration of emancipation was the last alternative, that it was "a military necessity absolutely essential to the preservation of the Union." Because the slaves were a tremendous source of strength for the rebellion, Lincoln must invite them to desert and "come to us and uniting with us they must be made free from rebel authority and rebel masters." His interview with the border men yesterday, he said, "had forced him slowly but he believed correctly to this conclusion."

On July 22, 1862, Lincoln summoned his cabinet members and read them a draft of a preliminary Emancipation Proclamation. Come January 1, 1863, in his capacity as commander-in-chief of the armed forces in time of war, Lincoln would free all the slaves everywhere in the rebel states. He would thus make it a Union objective to annihilate slavery as an institution in the Confederate South.

Contrary to what many historians have said, Lincoln's projected Proclamation went further than anything Congress had done. True, Congress had just enacted (and Lincoln had just signed) the second confiscation act, which provided for the seizure and liberation of all slaves of people who supported or participated in the rebellion. Still, most slaves would be freed only after protracted case-by-case litigation in the federal courts. Another section of the act did liberate certain categories of slaves without court action, but the bill exempted loyal slaveowners in the rebel South, allowing them to keep their slaves and other property. Lincoln's Proclamation, on the other hand, was a sweeping blow against bondage as an institution in the rebel states, a blow that would free *all* the slaves there—those of secessionists and loyalists alike. Thus Lincoln would handle emancipation himself, avoid judicial red tape, and use the military to vanquish the cornerstone of the Confederacy. Again, he justified this as a military necessity to save the Union.

But Seward and other cabinet secretaries dissuaded Lincoln from issuing his Proclamation in July. Seward argued that the Union had won no clear military victories, particularly in the showcase Eastern theater. As a consequence, Europe would misconstrue the Proclamation as "our last shriek on the retreat," as a wild and reckless attempt to compensate for Union military ineptitude by provoking a slave insurrection behind rebel lines. If Lincoln must give an emancipation order, Seward warned, he must wait until the Union won a military victory.

Lincoln finally agreed to wait, but he was not happy about it: the way George B. McClellan and his other generals had been fighting in the Eastern theater, Lincoln had no idea when he would ever have a victory.

One of the great ironies of the war was that McClellan presented Lincoln with the triumph he needed. A Democrat who sympathized with Southern slavery and opposed wartime emancipation with a passion, McClellan outfought Robert E. Lee at Antietam Creek in September 1862, and drove the rebel army from the battlefield. Thereupon Lincoln issued his preliminary Proclamation, with its warning that if the rebellion did not cease by January 1, 1863, the executive branch, including the army and the navy, would destroy slavery in the rebel states.

As it turned out, the preliminary Proclamation ignited racial discontent in much of the lower North, especially the Midwest, and led to a Republican disaster in the fall by-elections of 1862. Already Northern Democrats were upset with Lincoln's harsh war measures, especially his use of martial law and military arrests. But Negro emancipation was more than they could stand, and they stumped the Northern states that fall, beating the drums of Negrophobia, warning of massive influxes of Southern blacks into the North once emancipation came. Sullen, war weary, and racially aroused, Northern voters dealt the Republicans a smashing blow, as the North's five most populous states—all of which had gone for Lincoln in 1860—now returned Democratic majorities to

Congress. While the Republicans narrowly retained control of Congress, the future looked bleak indeed for 1864.

Republican analysts—and Lincoln himself—conceded that the preliminary Proclamation was a major factor in the Republican defeat. But Lincoln told a delegation from Kentucky that he would rather die than retract a single word in his Proclamation.

As the New Year approached, conservative Republicans begged Lincoln to abandon his "reckless" emancipation scheme lest he shatter their demoralized party and wreck what remained of their country. But Lincoln stood firm. On New Year's day, 1863, he officially signed the final Emancipation Proclamation in the White House. His hand trembled badly, not because he was nervous, but because he had shaken hands all morning in a White House reception. He assured everyone present that he was never more certain of what he was doing. "If my name ever goes into history," he said, "it will be for this act." Then slowly and deliberately he wrote out his full name.

In the final Proclamation, Lincoln temporarily exempted occupied Tennessee and certain occupied places in Louisiana and Virginia. (Later, in reconstructing those states, he withdrew the exemptions and made emancipation a mandatory part of his reconstruction program.) He also excluded the loyal slave states because they were not in rebellion and he lacked the legal authority to uproot slavery there. He would, however, keep goading them to obliterate slavery themselves—and would later push a constitutional amendment that liberated their slaves as well. With the exception of the loyal border and certain occupied areas, the final Proclamation declared that as of this day, all slaves in the rebellious states were "forever free." The document also asserted that black men—Southern and Northern alike—would now be enlisted in Union military forces.

Out the Proclamation went to an anxious and dissident nation. Later in the day an interracial crowd gathered on the White House lawn, and Lincoln greeted the people from an open window. The blacks cheered and sang, "Glory, Jubilee has come," and told Lincoln that if he would "come out of that palace, they would hug him to death." A black preacher named Henry M. Turner exclaimed that "it is indeed a time of times," that "nothing like it will ever be seen again in this life."

VI

Lincoln's Proclamation was the most revolutionary measure ever to come from an American president up to that time. As Union armies punched into rebel territory, they would rip out slavery as an institution, automatically freeing all slaves in the areas and states they conquered. In this respect (as Lincoln said), the war brought on changes more vast, more fundamental and profound, than either side had expected when the struggle began. Now slavery would perish as the Confederacy perished, would die by degrees with every Union advance, every Union victory.

Moreover, word of the Proclamation hummed across the slave grapevine in the Confederacy; and as Union armies drew near, more slaves than ever abandoned rebel farms and plantations and (as one said) "demonstrated with their feet" their desire for freedom.

The Proclamation also opened the army to black volunteers, and Northern free Negroes and Southern ex-slaves now enlisted as Union soldiers. As Lincoln said, "the colored population is the great *available* and yet unavailed of, force for restoring the Union." And he now availed himself of that force. In all, some 180,000 Negro fighting men—most of them emancipated slaves—served in Union forces on every major battle front, helping to liberate their brothers and sisters in bondage and to save the Union. As Lincoln observed, the blacks added enormous and indispensable strength to the Union war machine.

Unhappily, the blacks fought in segregated units under white officers, and until late in the war received less pay than whites did. In 1864 Lincoln told Frederick Douglass that he disliked the practice of unequal pay, but that the government had to make some concessions to white prejudices, noting that a great many Northern whites opposed the use of black soldiers altogether. But he promised that they would eventually get equal pay—and they did. Moreover, Lincoln was proud of the performance of his black soldiers: he publicly praised them for fighting "with clenched teeth, and steady eye, and well poised bayonet" to save the Union, while certain whites strove "with malignant heart" to hinder it.

After the Proclamation, Lincoln had to confront the problem of race adjustment, of what to do with all the blacks liberated in the South. By the spring of 1863, he had pretty well written off colonization as unworkable. His colonization schemes all floundered, in part because the white promoters were dishonest or incompetent. But the main reason colonization failed was because most blacks adamantly refused to participate in Lincoln's voluntary program. Across the North, free Negroes denounced Lincoln's colonization efforts—this was their country too! they cried—and they petitioned him to deport slaveholders instead.

As a consequence, Lincoln had just about concluded that whites and liberated blacks must somehow learn how to live together in this country. Still, he needed some device for now, some program that would pacify white Northerners and convince them that Southern freedmen would not flock into their communities, but would remain in the South instead. What Lincoln worked out was a refugee system, installed by his adjutant general in the occupied Mississippi Valley, which mobilized Southern blacks in the South, utilizing them in military and civilian pursuits there. According to the system, the adjutant general enrolled all able-bodied freedmen in the army, employed other ex-slaves as military laborers, and hired still others to work on farms and plantations for wages set by the government. While there were many faults with the system, it was predicated on sound Republican dogma: it kept Southern Negroes out of the North, and it got them jobs as wage earners, thus helping them to help themselves and preparing them for life in a free society.

Even so, emancipation remained the most explosive and unpopular act of Lincoln's presidency. By mid-1863, thousands of Democrats were in open revolt against his administration, denouncing Lincoln as an abolitionist dictator who had surrendered to radicalism. In the Midwest, dissident Democrats launched a peace movement to throw "the shrieking abolitionist faction" out of office and negotiate a peace with the Confederacy that would somehow restore the Union with slavery unharmed. There were large antiwar rallies against Lincoln's war for slave liberation. Race and draft riots flared in several Northern cities.

With all the public unrest behind the lines, conservative Republicans beseeched Lincoln to abandon emancipation and rescue his country "from the brink of ruin." But Lincoln seemed intractable. He had made up his mind to smash the slave society of the rebel South and eliminate "the cruel wrong" of Negro bondage, and no amount of public discontent, he indicated, was going to change his mind. "To use a coarse, but an expressive figure," he wrote one aggravated Democrat, "broken eggs cannot be mended. I have issued the Proclamation, and I cannot retract it." Congressman Owen Lovejoy applauded Lincoln's stand. "His mind acts slowly," Lovejoy said, "but when he moves, it is *forward.*"

He wavered once—in August 1864, a time of unrelenting gloom for Lincoln when his popularity had sunk to an all-time low and it seemed he could not be reelected. He confessed that maybe the country would no longer sustain a war for slave emancipation, that maybe he shouldn't pull the nation down a road it did not want to travel. On August 24 he decided to offer Jefferson Davis peace terms that excluded emancipation as a condition, vaguely suggesting that slavery would be adjusted later "by peaceful means." But the next day Lincoln changed his mind. With awakened resolution, he vowed to fight the war through to unconditional surrender and to stick by emancipation come what may. He had made his promise of freedom to the slaves, and he meant to keep it so long as he was in office.

When he won the election of 1864, Lincoln interpreted it as a popular mandate for him and his emancipation policy. But in reality the election provided no clear referendum on slavery, since Republican campaigners had played down emancipation and concentrated on the peace plank in the Democratic platform. Nevertheless, Lincoln used his reelection to promote a constitutional amendment that would guarantee the freedom of all slaves, those in the loyal border as well as those in the rebel South. Since issuing his Proclamation, Lincoln had worried that it might be nullified in the courts or thrown out by a later Congress or a subsequent administration. Consequently he wanted a constitutional amendment that would safeguard his Proclamation and prevent emancipation from ever being overturned.

As it happened, the Senate in May of 1864 had already passed an emancipation amendment—the present Thirteenth Amendment—but the House had failed to approve it. After that Lincoln had insisted that the Republican platform endorse the measure. And now, over the winter of 1864 and 1865, he put tremendous pressure on the House to endorse the amendment, using all his powers of persuasion and patronage to get it through. He buttonholed conservative Republicans and opposition Democrats and exhorted them to support the amendment. He singled out "sinners" among the Democrats who were "on praying ground," and informed them that they had a lot better chance for the federal jobs they desired if they voted for the measure. Soon two Democrats swung over in favor of it. With the outcome still in doubt, Lincoln participated in secret negotiations never made public—negotiations that allegedly involved the patronage, a New Jersey railroad monopoly, and the release of rebels related to Congressional Democrats—to bring wavering opponents into line. "The greatest measure of the nineteenth century," Thaddeus Stevens claimed, "was passed by corruption, aided and abetted by the purest man in America." On January 31, 1865, the House adopted the present Thirteenth Amendment by just three votes more than the required two-thirds majority. At once a storm of cheers broke over House Republicans, who danced around, embraced one another, and waved their hats and canes overhead. "It seemed to me I had been born with a new life," Julian recalled, "and that the world was overflowing with beauty and joy."

Lincoln, too, pronounced the amendment "a great moral victory" and "a King's cure" for the evils of slavery. When ratified by the states, the amendment would end human bondage everywhere in America. Lincoln pointed across the Potomac. "If the people over the river had behaved themselves, I could not have done what I have."

VII

Lincoln conceded, though, that he had not controlled the events of the war, but that events had controlled him instead, that God had controlled him. He thought about this a great deal, especially at night when he couldn't sleep, trying to understand the meaning of the war, to understand why it had begun and grown into such a massive revolutionary struggle, consuming hundreds of thousands of lives (the final casualties would come to 618,000 on both sides). By his second inaugural, he had reached an apocalyptic conclusion about the nature of the war—had come to see it as a divine punishment for the "great offense" of slavery, as a terrible retribution God had visited on a guilty people, in North as well as South. Lincoln's vision was close to that of old John Brown, who had prophesied on the day he was hanged, on that balmy December day back in 1859, that the crime of slavery could not be purged away from this guilty land except by blood. Now, in his second Inaugural Address, Lincoln too contended that God perhaps had willed this "mighty scourge of War" on the United States, "until all the wealth piled by the bondman's two hundred and fifty years of unrequited toil shall be sunk, and until every drop of blood drawn with the lash, shall be paid by another drawn from the sword."

In the last paragraph of his address, Lincoln said he would bind the nation's wounds "with malice toward none" and "charity for all." Yet that did not mean he would be so gentle and forgiving in reconstruction as most biographers have contended. He would be magnanimous in the sense that he wouldn't resort to mass executions or even mass imprisonment of Southern "traitors," as he repeatedly called them. He would not even have the leaders tried and jailed, though he said he would like to "frighten them out of the country." Nevertheless, still preoccupied with the war as a grim purgation which would cleanse and regenerate his country, Lincoln endorsed a fairly tough policy toward the conquered South. After Lee surrendered in April 1865, Lincoln publicly endorsed limited suffrage for Southern blacks, announcing that the intelligent ex-slaves and especially those who had served in Union military forces should have the vote. This put him in advance of most Northern whites. And it put him ahead of most Republicans as well—including many of the so-called radicals—who in April 1865 shrank from Negro suffrage out of fear of their own white constituents. True, Sumner, Salmon Chase, and a few of their colleagues now demanded that all Southern black men be enfranchised in order to protect their freedom. But Lincoln was not far from their position. In a line in his last political speech, April 11, 1865, he granted that the Southern black man deserved the vote, though Lincoln was not quite ready to make that mandatory. But it seems clear in what direction he was heading.

Moreover, in a cabinet meeting on Good Friday, 1865, Lincoln and all his Secretaries endorsed the military approach to reconstruction and conceded that an army of occupation might be necessary to control the rebellious white majority in the conquered South. During the war, Lincoln had always thought the military indispensable in restoring civilian rule in the South. Without the army, he feared that the rebellious Southern majority would overwhelm the small Unionist minority there—and maybe even re-enslave the blacks. And he was not about to let the latter happen. The army had liberated the blacks in the war, and the army might well have to safeguard their freedom in reconstruction.

VIII

He had come a long distance from the young Lincoln who entered politics, quiet on slavery lest he be branded an abolitionist, opposed to Negro political rights lest his political career be jeopardized, convinced that only the future could remove slavery in America. He had come a long way indeed. Frederick Douglass, who interviewed Lincoln in the White House in 1863, said he was "the first great man that I talked with in the United States freely who in no single instance reminded me of the difference between himself and myself, of the difference of color." Douglass, reflecting back on Lincoln's presidency, recalled how in the first year and a half of the war, Lincoln "was ready and willing" to sacrifice black people for the benefit and welfare of whites. But since the preliminary Emancipation Proclamation, Douglass said, American blacks had taken Lincoln's measure and had come to admire and some to love this enigmatic man. Though Lincoln had taxed Negroes to the limit, they had decided, in the roll and tumble of events, that "the how and the man of our redemption had somehow met in the person of Abraham Lincoln."

But perhaps it was Lincoln himself who best summed up his journey to emancipation—his own as well as that of the slaves. In December 1862, after the calamitous by-elections of that year, in the midst of rising racial protest against his emancipation policy, Lincoln asked Congress—and Northern whites beyond—for their support. "The dogmas of the quiet past," he reminded them, "are inadequate to the stormy present. The occasion is piled high with difficulty, and we must rise with the occasion. As our case is new, so we must think anew, and act anew. We must disenthrall our selves, and then we shall save our country.

"Fellow-citizens, *we* cannot escape history. . . . The fiery trial through which we pass, will light us down, in honor or dishonor, to the latest generation. . . . In *giving* freedom to the slave, we *assure* freedom to the *free*—honorable alike in what we give, and what we preserve. We shall nobly save, or meanly lose, the last best, hope of earth."

SEVEN

THE LONG SHADOW OF LINCOLN

I

AUTHENTIC contemporary accounts have an enduring value both as history and as literature. Though they may have been written a century or even a thousand years ago, they remain vividly alive, timeless recordings of historical events as seen through the eyes of people who witnessed and often shaped them. That is why Quadrangle's new edition of three Lincoln source books—Herbert Mitgang, ed., *Abraham Lincoln, A Press Portrait;* Edward Dicey, *Spectator of America* (until now never published in the United States); and Noah Brooks, *Washington, D.C., in Lincoln's Time*—has a special appeal for us today. The books provide a fascinating, eyewitness view of wartorn America, enabling us to experience that troubled time as though it were our own. They afford rare glimpses of Lincoln, too, who emerges as a beleaguered, humanized president who suffered one of the worst presses of any chief executive in American history.

In truth, those with a repugnance for journalism will find plenty in *Abraham Lincoln, A Press Portrait,* to vindicate their feelings. A compendium of press clippings by and about Lincoln, the volume contains editorials from seven magazines and seventy-eight newspapers, including ten foreign journals. All are arranged chronologically from Lincoln's early years down to his assassination, with italicized introductions to facilitate transitions. The result is not so much a portrait of Lincoln as an exposure of nineteenth-century American journalism—a journalism that was intemperate, pugnacious, and fanatically partisan. Some of the reportage gathered here is reasonable enough—Harriet Beecher Stowe's assessment of Lincoln is especially thoughtful. But many of the other editorials are mindlessly abusive, intended less to inform than to agitate their readers. In 1859, for example, an Ohio Democratic paper had this to say about a Lincoln address on slavery and sectionalism: "We do not say that we have read it: it is not worth reading. It contains nothing that is calculated to make any man wiser, or more learned; to make him a better citizen or a better man; to give him any insight into the character of the Government. . . . It is, in a single expressive word, *trash*— trash from beginning to end; trash without one solitary oasis to relieve the dreary waste that begins with its nearest and ends with its furthest boundary." When Lincoln won the Republican nomination in 1860, a rival Republican journal bemoaned "his coarse language, his illiterate style, and his vulgar and vituperative personalities in debate," and argued that "there is not in all the history of his life any exhibition of intellectual ability and attainments fitting him for the high and responsible post in the Government for which he has been nominated."

The most savage editorials appeared in Southern journals like the Charleston *Mercury* and the New Orleans *Daily Picayune*. By turns, they castigated Lincoln as "an Ourang-outang" with "an eye for a pretty girl," as "Jackson the Deuce," as "a black-hearted fanatic" who lusted for Negro equality. The *Mercury* even blasted Lincoln's conciliatory first Inaugural Address—with its approval of the original Thirteenth Amendment—as an open declaration of war. "King LINCOLN," the paper ranted, "Rail Splitter ABRA-HAM—Imperator! We thank thee for this. It is the tocsin of battle, but it is the signal of our freedom. Quickly, oh quickly begin the fray. Haste to levy tribute. 'Enforce the laws' with all possible speed! We have no money to pay, but we have treasure enough— liquid wealth, redder than any gold and infinitely more precious. Be sure, be very sure, O! low-born, despicable tyrant, that the price of liberty will be paid—good measure, heaped up, shaken down, running over, in hot streams fresh from hearts that will not, cannot beat in the breasts of slaves."

Similar anti-Lincoln invective inhabited the pages of the Chicago *Times*, the New York *Herald*, and the New York *Daybook*, which inveighed against Lincoln's "Negro Republican Administration" and flayed away at the Emancipation Proclamation "as a monstrous usurpation, a criminal wrong, and an act of national suicide." The *Herald*, in a display of lurid condemnation, described a Lincoln meeting in 1864 as "one of the most disgraceful exhibitions of human depravity ever witnessed in this wicked world. It was a gathering of ghouls, vultures, hyenas and other feeders upon carrion, for the purpose of surfeiting themselves upon the slaughter of the recent battles. ... The great ghoul at Washington, who authorized the meeting, and the little ghouls and vultures who conducted it, have succeeded in completely disgusting the people of this country."

When Lincoln was renominated in 1864, the *Illinois State Register* decried his "ambition and arrogance" and proclaimed that "the most powerful monarchy in Europe would not *dare* commit the outrages which have been put upon us by the Lincoln administration." In an editorial not included in *Abraham Lincoln, A Press Portrait*, an opposition paper in Wisconsin flatly declared, "If Abraham Lincoln should be re-elected for another term of four years of such wretched administration, *we hope that a bold hand will be found to plunge the dagger into the Tyrant's heart for the public welfare.*" Even more shocking was the statement that appeared in the Houston *Tri-Weekly Telegraph* after Lincoln was assassinated. "From now until God's judgment day, the minds of men will not cease to thrill at the killing of Abraham Lincoln."

Reading through this collection of journalism will tell you a great deal about the Civil War era. For if English traveler Edward Dicey was right, if "the American must be defined as a newspaper-reading animal," then the American press, with all its petulance and vitriol, deserves some of the blame for the violent passions which divided Americans in Lincoln's time.

II

In sharp contrast to the acrimony that pervades *Abraham Lincoln, A Press Portrait*, Dicey's own reportage is open-minded and gracefully written. Educated at Trinity College, Cambridge, Dicey was a young writer for *The Spectator* and *Macmillan's Magazine*. In 1862, he visited America to find out for himself what the Civil War was about. For six months he rode slow, rattling trains from

New York out to St. Louis and back East again, and then went home to publish his impressions. His book is a marvelous work of art, alive with the people—the sights, sounds, and smells—of Civil War America, all narrated with a perceptiveness reminiscent of Alexis de Tocqueville. Here are trenchant observations of American journalism: "The American papers have not learnt yet the difference between declamation and strong writing, and, therefore, their attacks on political enemies are perfectly astonishing to us for the violence of their invective." Yet "even in declamations against public men, allusions to their private relations are but rare" and "attacks on individuals in private life are almost unknown." Unlike England, Dicey wryly noted, American public opinion "is opposed to raking up the private affairs of individuals for the amusement of newspaper readers; and the newspapers do not publish the gossip of the police courts, simply because the public does not wish for it."

As for the manners and mores of Americans, Dicey found them a "frank and congenial" people always anxious to please. Yet their society was marred by a disconcerting uniformity, Dicey thought, a sameness in their opinions, speech, culture, and architecture that bothered him. New York he found dreadfully monotonous, with its plain streets, rows of stunted trees, and redundant, undistinguished buildings, which betrayed a lack of "artistic taste." Still, there was a serenity about New York which Dicey had never seen in European cities. And he noticed that "in this crisp, clear air, there is a sort of French sparkle about the place which enlivens it strangely."

From New York, Dicey takes us on a railroad journey down to Washington, D.C. He seats himself in a long, open car with a wide aisle in the middle, settling on horsehair or leather cushions as the train grinds out of the station with bells clanging. The day goes by "not unpleasantly," although Dicey discovers that Americans—in contrast to Europeans—"are not a communicative people in traveling." Everyone "is quiet, well-behaved, and civil; and there is little or nothing of that offensive selfishness so often exhibited amongst English travelers in the attempt to make oneself comfortable at the expense of everybody else's discomfort." He is struck, too, at how polite American men are to women. "If a woman enters the car, and the car is full, some gentleman or other is sure to get up and make room for her. It is no matter whether she is young or old, pretty or ugly, richly or poorly dressed, she is a woman, and that suffices."

Every half-hour a boy passes through the car with a can of ice water, and you can have a free glass, if you don't object to drinking after others. At other times, the boy peddles oranges, apples, sweets, and the latest issues of magazines and papers. Here Dicey perceives "an odd trait" in the national character. The young vendor would lay a copy of a magazine or illustrated paper beside each passenger and leave it for an hour or so. There is nothing to stop someone from appropriating the work without paying for it, yet nobody does. "In this, as in other matters, it is the custom to repose great confidence on the average honesty of the public, and that confidence is rarely found to have been misplaced."

Three times a day the train stops at some roadside station for meals. They are the same everywhere regardless of the time. "You eat plentifully of beefsteaks, broiled ham, poached eggs, pastry without end, and cakes; drink milk, or tea, or water—never beer or any spiritous liquors; are waited on by neat, clean-looking girls; liquor afterward at the bars." Then you take your seat again and sleep or read or talk until the next feeding time, and so the day passes.

As the train leaves Pennsylvania and puffs into slaveholding Maryland, "the whole aspect of the scenery changes: the broad, thriving cheerful expanse of carefully tilled fields, dotted over with the villa-like farm houses, gives place to long, straggling, red brick towns, half villages, half cities; to broken-down fences; to half-ploughed, hopeless-looking fields; where the Negro laborers are toiling listlessly; to dreary tracks of mud, which stand where roads ought to be; and to wide stony spaces of meager brushwood."

Dicey is even more unimpressed with Washington, which strikes him as "an overgrown watering place." The city "looks run up in a night, like the cardboard cities which Potemkin erected to gratify the eyes of his imperial mistress on her tour through Russia; and it is impossible to remove the impression that, when Congress is over, the whole place is taken down, and packed up again till wanted." And the hotels are abominations. "Willard's and the National are two huge rambling barracks where some incredible number of beds could be run up; but it is hard to say which is the shabbier and dirtier internally; and externally, neither of them have any pretensions to architectural grandeur. Of the lot, Willard's is the best, on the principle that if you are to eat your peck of dirt, you may as well eat it in as picturesque a form as possible." The worst thing about Washington, though, was the weather. "On a fine bright day, when the wooded banks that line the south side of the Potomac were in their early bloom, I have thought the city looked wondrously light; but on nine days out of every ten the climate of Washington is simply detestable. When it rains, the streets are sloughs of liquid mud; and, by some miraculous peculiarity I could never get accounted for, even in the paved streets the stones sink into the ground and the mud oozes up between them. In a couple of hours from the time the rain ceases, the same streets are enveloped in clouds of dust. In springtime, the contrast between the burning sun and the freezing winds is greater than I ever knew it in Italy; and in summer, the heat is more dead and oppressive than in any place it has been my lot to dwell in."

What saves Washington from being the ugliest capital in the world, he decides, are the two marble palaces of the Capitol Building and the Treasury, "frowning at each other like old German castles." The Capitol is still under construction, with lumber and blocks of unhewn marble strewn about the grounds. And the unfinished dome, visible from miles away, is a framework of girders and beams, surmounted by a crane. "Like everything in America," Dicey says, "the whole building is new, painfully so." Inside, he wanders "through endless passages, and richly roofed corridors, and stately staircases," until at last he comes to the great central hall, honeycombed with scaffolds, where historical pictures are on display. A portrait of James Buchanan, Lincoln's "dough face" predecessor, once hung here, but at the start of the war a Western regiment defaced the portrait by spitting tobacco juice all over it. "And a vile indignity, too, sir, that was," said an abolitionist who told Dicey the story, "for the tobacco juice."

In the main passages, fruit stands sell fruit, nuts, and lager beer to the public, while congressional refreshment rooms cater to thirsty politicians, who share war news over whiskey and brandy cocktails. Going down the echoing hallways, Dicey comes to the galleries of the great Hall of Representatives, a resplendent, rectangular room filled with legislators at their work. Dicey is startled at the air of casual indifference that pervades the House floor. "The scene looks like a lecture room where the class is paying no attention to the lecturer. Some of the members, not many, have their legs sprawling over the desks; some are sleeping in their chairs; and the majority are writing or reading, or talking in low voices to their neighbors." Most of them appear to be business-men, "slightly bored at an unprofitable waste of time." The de-meanor of the House, then, is more staid than that of Parliament, and "the only distinct sound which interrupts the somewhat droning tones of the orators' voices is the constant clap-clap of the members' hands, as they summon the boy-pages to run on errands." Still, Dicey is quite taken with the fluency of the speak-ers. "Everybody has the gift of speaking—the power, at least, of stringing words together without a hitch. I never heard an Amer-ican member of either House stutter, or hem and haw, as nineteen-twentieths of our speakers do when in want of a word."

As he ingratiated himself with Washington politicians, listen-ing to all the talk and gossip around him, Dicey learned how unpopular Abraham Lincoln was in the darkening months of 1862. With the war going badly for the Union, everybody regarded him as a failure and said so "with an almost brutal frankness." In-terviewing Lincoln himself, Dicey found the president "a shrewd hard-headed, self-educated man, with sense enough to perceive his own deficiencies, but without the instinctive genius which supplies the place of learning. . . . He works hard, and does little; and unites a painful sense of responsibility to a still more painful sense, perhaps, that his work is too great for him to grapple with."

Physically, Dicey noted, Lincoln was thin and awkward, with "uncombed and uncombable" black hair, a narrow chest, and long and bony limbs that always seemed in the way. His mouth was stern and his face furrowed and wrinkled, and his eyes, sunken behind bushy brows, gazed dreamily "through you without look-ing at you." Yet Lincoln was strong and strangely dignified, with a "complete absence of pretension" and an "evident desire to be courteous to everybody, which is the essence, if not the outward form, of high breeding." The president also had a sad smile and a "dry Yankee humor, not inconsistent . . . with a sort of habitual melancholy." When he related an anecdote, Lincoln would chuckle and rub his hand down the side of his leg. But he could be reflective, too, and spoke at one point about American orators. "It is very common in this country to find great facility of expression, and common, though not so common, to find great lucidity of thought. The combination of the two faculties in one person is uncommon indeed; but whenever you do find it, you have a great man."

From Washington, Dicey headed out across America, his eyes taking in the people and the sights like "a magnifying camera." He visited the front lines in Virginia, journeyed into Kentucky and Tennessee, and crossed the windy prairies to Chicago, "Queen City of the West," which he thought the most striking of America's business cities with its music and book shops and refined homes. On his travels, he recorded graphic descriptions of the German influences on St. Louis and of the Old World demeanor of Boston and Cambridge. And he gathered impressions of slavery and slaveowners, too, reporting how the latter repeatedly told him that their Negroes were happy and contented and did not want freedom. "It may be so," Dicey said, "but if so, it is hard to explain why the papers of the Slave States are filled with advertisements of runaway slaves."

Above all, Dicey perceived that slavery and the place of the Negro were the paramount issues in Lincoln's America. At a time when most Europeans were puzzled about the nature of the Civil War, Dicey clearly understood that "slavery is the one cause of Secession." Yet he also perceived that Northern whites were hardly warm-hearted abolitionists, that most of them combined "a very genuine dislike for slavery and a readiness to make sacrifices for Abolition, with an extreme distaste for any kind of connection or amalgamation with the free Negro." He went on: "It is hard for a European to quite appreciate the intensity of American feeling about color; but still, when an American asks you the usual question, whether you would like your sister to marry a Negro, I own that candor would force most Englishmen to answer in the negative. A black brother can be tolerated, but a black brother-in-law is an idea not pleasant to the Anglo-Saxon mind."

Still, Dicey loathed slavery and wrote about it with a searing frankness: slavery "has one peculiar guilt, which few, if any other of the hundred modes of human cruelty and oppression, can be justly charged with. It is a gigantic, almost an isolated, attempt to reduce oppression to a system, and to establish a social order

of which the misery of human beings is the fundamental principle. It is for this reason that every honest man, who hates cruelty
and loves justice, is bound to lift up his voice against slavery as
an accursed thing."

And Dicey lifted up his voice clearly and eloquently for the
North against the South, for he thought a Union victory would
mean the death of slavery. And so, he informed his countrymen
after his return, "in the interest of humanity, in the interest of
America, and in the interest of England, the success of the North
is the thing we ought to hope and wish for."

III

Like Dicey, correspondent Noah Brooks was also a keen observer,
a journalist who went against the currents of bigotry and narrow-
mindedness that prevailed in his time. A native of Castine, Maine,
Brooks entered journalism at the age of twenty and eventually
migrated to California, where he helped publish a pro-Republican
newspaper. In 1862, he went to Washington as war correspondent
for the Sacramento *Daily Union*, for which he wrote a total of 258
dispatches signed "Castine." In Washington, he became a trusted
friend of the Lincolns, visited the White House regularly, and did
all he could to help the president: he supplied Lincoln with information about Congress, California politics and personalities, and
the 1864 nominating conventions. And in the spring of 1865 he
agreed to become Lincoln's personal secretary, though he never
got a chance to serve. Thirty years later, after an erratic career as
a journalist in California and New Jersey, Brooks recorded his
Civil War experiences in *Washington in Lincoln's Time*, based
partly on memory and partly on his own war correspondence.

The book became a classic—a major source from that time on
not only about the lives of the president and his family, but about
events in wartime Washington as well. A gifted writer with an eye
for detail, Brooks wrote of "the frowning fortifications that en-
closed Washington," of the ubiquitous hospitals and barracks, of
"the long lines of army wagons and artillery" rumbling through
the streets by night and by day, and of the "squalid Negro quarters" that "hung on the flanks of fine old mansions."

He wrote, too, about the leaders in Congress, and some of his vignettes are remarkable. He said of Thaddeus Stevens: "He spoke with great calmness and deliberation, dropping his sentences as though each weighed a ton," and "he launched his anathemas at his opponents as coolly as if he were bandying compliments." And of Henry Winter Davis, Lincoln's antagonist in the House: "At that time he was about forty-five years of age, light in complexion, with a round, boyish head, sandy hair and mustache. He had a high, clear, ringing voice, and a manner of speaking which was peculiar in his sharpness and firmness. . . . Garfield once said of him that his eloquence was 'clear and cold, like starlight.' " And of Charles Sumner: "He once told me that he never allowed himself, even in the privacy of his own chamber, to fall into a position which he would not take in his chair in the Senate. 'Habit,' he said, 'is everything.' " Brooks added: "In the rear of Sumner's [Washington] apartment was a gallery from which the interior of the rooms could be viewed. The younger members of the Gardner family, with a curiosity natural to youth, would be attracted by the sound of the Senator's magnificent voice rehearsing his speech, and from the gallery they could look in and see him before a pier-glass, fixed between the front windows, studying the effect of his gestures by the light of lamps placed at each side of the mirror."

Brooks's best writing, though, was about Lincoln himself—his daily activities, his moods, memory, intelligence, and eating and reading habits—all presented with a judicious mixture of detachment and sympathy. No legend-builder, Brooks depicted Lincoln as a real-life human being who had faults as well as strengths, who could forget to eat, become distracted in thought, and lose his temper. When he learned of Lee's escape after Gettysburg, Brooks recalled, Lincoln's "grief and anger were something sorrowful to behold."

Through Brooks's eyes, we see the president mobbed by office-seekers, watch him endure the ordeal of public receptions, and accompany him on his nocturnal walks to and from the War Department. Once, in deference to Mary and her worries about his safety, Lincoln carried a wooden stick for protection. But he told Brooks there wasn't much he could do to ward off assassination. "I long ago made up my mind that if anybody wants to kill me, he will do it. If I wore a shirt of mail, and kept myself surrounded by a body-guard, it would be all the same. There are a thousand ways of getting at a man if it is desired that he should be killed."

In the chill spring days of 1863, we go with Lincoln down to Falmouth Station in Virginia, to review General George Hooker's Army of the Potomac. "The cavalcade on the way from headquarters to the reviewing-field was a brilliant one," Brooks writes. "The President, wearing a high hat and riding like a veteran, with General Hooker by his side, headed the flying column.... The uneven ground was soft with melting snow, and the mud flew in every direction under the hurrying feet of the cavalcade. On the skirts of this cloud of cavalry rode the President's little son 'Tad,' in charge of a mounted orderly, his gray cloak flying in the gusty wind like the plume of Henry of Navarre." Then the President stopped to watch the cavalry march by in review. "It was a grand sight to look upon, this immense body of cavalry, with banners waving, music crashing, and horses prancing, as the vast column came winding like a huge serpent over the hills past the reviewing party, and then stretching far away out of sight."

During the visit, Lincoln toured the rancid hospital tents, shaking hands with the wounded "and asking a question or two here and there, and leaving a kind word as he moved from cot to cot." Accompanied by Tad and Brooks, the president also made his way down to the Rappahannock and peered across the river at Fredericksburg, where the Army of the Potomac suffered a disastrous defeat last December and where Lee's army was now encamped. Smoke from enemy camps rose from behind a ridge, and a rebel flag floated over a mansion on Marye's Heights, just above the stone wall where thousands of Union soldiers had died. Then Lincoln studied the town itself through a field glass. "The walls of the houses were rent with shot and shell, and loose sheets of tin were fluttering from the steeple of a church that had been in the line of fire. A tall chimney stood solitary by the river's brink, and on its bare and exposed hearthstone two rebel pickets were warming themselves."

Back at Washington, we catch a glimpse of Lincoln in the White House after Hooker lost the battle of Chancellorsville. "Never, as long as I knew him, did he seem to be so broken, so dispirited, and so ghostlike," Brooks records. "Clasping his hands behind his back, he walked up and down the room, saying, 'My God! my God! What will the country say! What will the country say!' "

After Lincoln removed Hooker from command, Brooks spoke with the deposed general in a Washington hotel room. The young journalist was sympathetic, for he considered Hooker, "by all odds, the handsomest soldier I ever laid eyes on." Crushed now and angry, the general stormed at his former subordinates and Secretary of War Edwin Stanton "as the authors of all his misfortunes." Still, Hooker admired Lincoln and had wanted desperately to please him. What, he asked Brooks, did the president say about him? "I hesitated, but when he pressed for a reply, said that Lincoln had told me that he regarded Hooker very much as a father might regard a son who was lame, or who had some other incurable physical infirmity. His love for his son would be even intensified by the reflection that the lad could never be a strong and successful man." When he heard that, Hooker got tears in his eyes.

As the narrative moves briskly along, we are with Lincoln on the day of his reelection and hear him deliver his second Inaugural Address under a cloudy sky. And we observe him on the misty evening of April 11, 1865, speaking of reconstruction and Negro suffrage "to a vast sea of faces, illuminated by the lights that burned in the festal array of the White House." In the chapter on "Life in the White House," we are told about Tad's escapades and about the president's own habits and eccentricities. We learn that Lincoln had a "Chinese reverence for written papers" and that he often carried his passion for written documents to the extreme. And we are given a surprisingly critical evaluation of Lincoln's intellect. In Brooks's opinion, the president had a lucid and rational mind, but he was no genius. His thinking was "acute rather than profound."

Brooks ends his story with a description of the last Grand Review in Washington, when more than 150,000 Union soldiers marched through the streets in brilliant May sunshine, guns gleaming and flags snapping in the wind as regiment after regiment tramped by to the music of fifes and drums. Then the pageant faded, the victorious Union army "melted back into the heart of the people from whence it came, and the great spectacle of the Grand Army of the Republic on review disappeared from sight."

And so one puts the book aside, the voices and scenes of Lincoln's America still lingering in one's mind. Because it is an authentic contemporary portrait of the Civil War and the troubled and visionary man who presided over it, Brooks's narrative—along with Dicey's *Spectator of America*—belongs on the bookshelves of everyone who likes the human side of history. Together, the two narratives vividly capture a tragic and cataclysmic era whose concussions are still being felt in our own time.

EIGHT

CARL SANDBURG'S LINCOLN

ANY attempt to discuss Carl Sandburg's six-volume *Abraham Lincoln* is like groping after elusive minnows. It is hard to get a focus on his work, to grasp exactly what it is. Is this biography or historical fiction? Is it an authentic life-and-times chronicle or a fact-and-fiction scenario—the literary equivalent of a Cecil B. DeMille spectacular? Is it really history—that is, a careful approximation of what Lincoln and his era were like? Or is it a potpourri of fact, invention, and folklore?

Even Sandburg found it difficult to describe his work. He told his editor Alfred Harcourt: "I think the Lincoln book will be a sort of History and Old Testament of the United States, a joke almanac, prayer collect, and compendium of essential facts." Later, as he struggled with the *War Years*, he wrote of its sprawling size: "This has grown into a scroll, a chronicle. There's one thing we can say for it: it is probably the only book ever written by a man whose father couldn't write his name, about a man whose mother couldn't write hers." And again, as he labored toward the end: "Sometimes I look at this damned vast manuscript and it seems just a memorandum I made for my own use in connection with a long adventure of reading, study and thought aimed at reaching into what actually went on in one terrific crisis—with occasional interpolations of meditations, sometimes musical, having to do with any and all human times." He was certain of one thing, though, and that was the symphonic quality of his story—of its "Sibelius bleakness and Bach repetition" that was so like the era itself.

Still, Sandburg could never quite define what he had created. And his critics could scarcely agree either. For historian Milo Quaife, Sandburg's *Lincoln* was sheer fiction, "a literary grab bag" which could never be acceptable as history. For Richard Hofstadter, it was a corpulent and "monumental bodying forth of the Lincoln legend." For Edmund Wilson, it was not only useless as a repository of folklore (because Sandburg himself contributed so much to the folklore), but was the "cruellest thing that has happened to Lincoln since he was shot by Booth." On the other hand, Stephen Vincent Benét considered Sandburg's *Lincoln* "a mountain range of biography." Robert E. Sherwood pronounced it "a monument that would stand forever" and declared that Sandburg wrote with "the poetic passion and the somber eloquence of the great masters of tragedy." More recently, North Callahan judged Sandburg's *Lincoln* a revolutionary work that "altered the conventional foundations of writing biography." And David Donald praised it as an "engrossing, warmly human portrait" that would likely never be superseded. Still, even Sandburg's most ardent supporters conceded that he had made a number of factual mistakes and had colored his story with a poet's imagination and license. Nevertheless, biographer Benjamin Thomas stoutly defended Sandburg's *Lincoln*, flaws and all, because it was a superb blend of imagination, reality, and idealism about the man Thomas called "Father Abraham." "The realist's ruthless searching gives the necessary facts," Thomas asserted. "Yet the realist is ill-advised to scorn the idealist's sensitivity to those soul qualities of Lincoln which documentary facts alone may not disclose."

As these quotations suggest, there are two kinds of truth involved in any consideration of Sandburg's *Lincoln*: biographical truth and mythical truth. If we are to grasp the elusive nature of his work, to assess fairly the soul qualities he ascribed to Lincoln, we must make a careful distinction between these two truths. With all respect for Sandburg's prodigious narrative and the years of toil required to compose it, I submit that it is not true biography. As the late Paul Murray Kendall correctly defined it, true biography is a unique province of literature whose mission is to "perpetuate a man as he was in the days he lived—a spring task of bringing to life again." Long on realism and short on romance, true biography resists the lure of fictional imaginings so as to be faithful to biographical art—to what actually happened. Any literary device which thrusts life-writing beyond the materials at hand ruptures biographical truth, Kendall contended. Thus there is science as well as art in true life-writing. In his research stage, the true biographer is as painstaking as any scientist in his pursuit of evidence. Wary and skeptical of witnesses, he plays them off against one another until he can corroborate some degree of accuracy. Then on the basis of authenticated detail, he begins to shape his portrait. Once he sets about the task of composition, however, the true biographer is an artist whose purpose is to rub his facts until they glow with human life. As Kendall observed, this excludes fictional biography, which creates life but not on the basis of tested evidence. This also excludes "critical," "interpretive," and fact-crammed biographies, which may respect the materials at hand but do not bring their subjects alive. Moreover, if the subject is truly heroic, he will emerge that way from authentic detail, from what he actually did and said. The subject needs no help from the biographer in reaching the mountain top.

By these standards, Sandburg's *Lincoln* is not true biography. The two-volume *Prairie Years*, for their part, abound with fictional passages—with dialogue, scenes, and thoughts the author simply made up. Though almost nothing is known about Lucy Hanks, Sandburg writes of her and baby Nancy: "She could croon in the moist evening twilight to the shining face in the sweet bundle, 'Hush thee, hush thee, thy father's a gentleman.' She could toss the bundle into the air against a far, hazy line of blue mountains, catch it in her two hands as it came down, let it snuggle to her breast and feed, while she asked, 'Here we come—where from?' " And after a night of sleep, "the tug of a mouth at her nipples in the grey dawn matched in its freshness the first warbling of birds and the morning stars." What is more, Sandburg repeats all manner of folk tales about young Lincoln and lets them stand as fact. He reports that Lincoln shucked corn "from early dawn till sundown" and then read books till midnight, that he kissed Green Taylor's girl, that he once fought William Grigsby and cried "I'm the big buck of this lick," that he lifted barefoot boys so they could leave muddy footprints on the ceiling of the Lincoln cabin, and that as a New Salem clerk he walked six miles to return a few cents a customer had overpaid on her bill. And Sandburg not only accepts the apocryphal story that Lincoln and Ann Rutledge were in love and planned to marry, but manufactures scenes about them. "After the first evening in which Lincoln had sat next to her and found that bashful words tumbling from his tongue's end really spelled themselves out into sensible talk, her face, as he went away, kept coming back. So often all else would fade out of his mind and there would be only this riddle of a pink-fair face, a mouth and eyes in a frame of light corn-silk hair. He could ask himself what it meant and search his heart for an answer and no answer would come. A trembling took his body and dark waves ran through him sometimes when she spoke so simple a thing as, 'The corn is getting high, isn't it?' " Which moved Edmund Wilson to remark, "The corn is getting high, indeed!" And then when Ann died, Sandburg's Lincoln is stricken with a lover's grief: he wanders absently in the forest; he makes his way to the burying ground outside New Salem and lies with an arm across Ann's grave. "In the evenings it was useless to try to talk with him," Sandburg continues. "He sat by the fire one night as the flames licked up the cordwood and swept up the chimney to pass out into a driving storm-wind. The blowing weather woke some sort of lights in him and he went to the door and looked out into a night of fierce tumbling wind and black horizons. And he came back saying, 'I can't bear to think of her out there alone.' And he clenched his hands, mumbling, 'The rain and the storm shan't beat on her grave.' " There is not a shred of evidence for any of this.

In fairness to Sandburg, he did delete a lot of this material in a one-volume condensation of the *Prairie* and *War Years*, published in 1954. But even there he persists in suggesting a love match between Ann and Lincoln and even quotes Edgar Lee Master's ridiculous poem about how Ann Rutledge, "beloved in life of Abraham Lincoln," was wedded to him in her grave.

There are many other dubious stories and imagined episodes in the *Prairie Years*, but let me turn to Sandburg's portrait of Lincoln himself. As he set to work on the book, Sandburg strongly identi-fied with his Lincoln and even dressed, acted, and physically re-sembled the figure he depicted. "Like him," Sandburg said, "I am a son of the prairie, a poor boy who wandered over the land to find himself and his mission in life." Like Sandburg, the Lin-coln of the *Prairie Years* is indigenously American, utterly shaped by the sprawling, unruly, pungent democracy of his day. He is simple, honest and ambitious, practical and wise. In his adult years, he is a homespun village lawyer and politician, dressed in a rumpled suit and a stovepipe hat, his head often bowed in melancholy. He is always relating anecdotes, though, and in the company of his male friends he can tell off-color stories and indulge in an expletive like "son-of-a-bitch." He is a flawed and yet mystic man, a thoroughly democratic individual distinguished for his wilderness humor and sagacity. Above all, his heart beats with the pulse of rural, working-class America, and he loves the common folk and revels in daily contact with them. But behind his bucolic plainness is a profound and mystical spirit awaiting its call to greatness. And that call, of course, comes in the grim and terrible years after 1854. Now Lincoln is a ghost on the platform, explaining to the people that the Revolution and freedom really mean something and reminding them of forgotten oaths and wasted sacrifices. In his great debates with Stephen A. Douglas, Lincoln is always one with the people, thrilling them with his "stubby, homely words." For the folk masses, he is both "the Strange Friend and Friendly Stranger." He is "like something out of a picture book for children"—tall, bony, comical, haunted-looking, and sad. Already stories about him are spreading among the plain folk, and many sit brooding and inquiring about this "fabulous human figure of their own time." By 1861, History has called him to his tragic destiny: his is "a mind, a spirit, a tongue, and a voice" for an American democracy caught in its greatest trial. As he leaves Illinois for Washington, the presidency, and the war years, voices cry out, "Good-bye, Abe."

This is, of course, the Lincoln of mythology, and Sandburg captures this Lincoln more vividly and consistently than any previous folk biographer. But for the sake of biographical truth, let us compare this mythical "Abe" Lincoln with the real-life man. Nowhere in the *Prairie Years* do we find the literate young Lincoln who became estranged from his father and left Thomas Lincoln's world—a rural world of mindless physical toil—and never returned. Nowhere do we glimpse the self-made attorney who had such superior legal talent and command of technical data that he became a lawyer's lawyer. Nowhere are we told that Lincoln did his most influential and fulfilling legal work, not on the circuit among country folk, but in the Illinois Supreme Court. Nowhere do we find the Lincoln who disliked the nickname "Abe" and went by "Mr. Lincoln" or just "Lincoln" even among his close friends. Nowhere are we told that the Lincoln of the 1840s and 1850s counted no farmers among his coterie of Springfield friends and had no interest in farming or sympathy for farm problems. Though Lincoln was exceedingly honest and fair-minded, with a deep commitment to the right of all people to elevate themselves, he was, as I've said elsewhere, a widely respected professional man and proud of it. In his younger years, moreover, he questioned who he was and worried about sexual matters, death, and madness. Yet this Lincoln, so complex and richly human, is hard to find in the *Prairie Years*.

What is more, nowhere in those volumes do we see the eloquent and visionary politician who extolled America's experiment in popular government—and the hope it held out to people the world over—more eloquently than anybody of his generation. Nowhere do we see the Lincoln who wanted a seat in the national Senate even more than the presidency itself, because in that august body he could defend the containment of slavery, defend the North's free-labor system, defend the Declaration of Independence, defend the right of Negroes to harvest the fruit of their labors, in speeches that would be widely read and preserved for posterity in the *Congressional Globe*. Nowhere from 1854 to 1860 do we hear Lincoln delivering speeches so lucid, so full of vivid imagery and nobility of thought, that they stand even today as examples of literary art. Nowhere do we glimpse the Lincoln who battled desperately to block what he thought was a Slave-Power conspiracy to nationalize slavery and overthrow popular government. Nowhere do we find the Lincoln who, accused again and again of desiring racial mongrelization, proclaimed anti-Negro sentiments in white-supremacist Illinois. In point of fact, Sandburg entirely omits Lincoln's remarks in the 1858 debates that he was not and never had been in favor of Negro social and political equality with white people. One supposes that Sandburg, himself a friend of the Negro and a champion of the underdog, could ill-afford to let his folk hero make concessions to a white-supremacist electorate, including the plain people themselves. Furthermore, Sandburg does not tell us that thousands of those plain folk voted for Douglas candidates in 1858 and helped return Lincoln's arch rival to the Senate. Nor does he tell us that most Americans in

1860 thought his people's hero too radical and dangerous to occupy the White House.

In the four-volume *War Years*, published thirteen years after the *Prairie Years*, Sandburg is more careful as a biographer. For the most part, he avoids fictional imaginings and adheres to an awesome mass of information he accumulated about the war and the man at its center. In a preface that resembles a prelude to a vast and epic symphony, Sandburg declares that the *War Years* present "events of wild passionate onrush side by side with cruel, grinding monotony." He recalls that "many men and women, now faded and gone, lived the book before it could be written," and warns that "what they say in words, within quotation marks, in these pages, is from sources deemed authentic, unless otherwise indicated." The result is a spectacular panorama, with Lincoln himself alternately disappearing and reappearing in a rush of crowded scenes and events. The book is full of the sound and fury—the blood and stench—of Civil War. And it captures all the immense confusion and tumult through which Lincoln day-by-day had to make his way. When we do see the president, in between extensive passages on military and political developments in North and South alike, he is entirely an external Lincoln. We scarcely ever view things through his eyes, scarcely ever feel his feelings—his anguish, sorrow, rage, and joy. No, the Lincoln of the *War Years* is an observed hero, filtered to us through the vision and sensibilities of hundreds of witnesses who called at his White House office, from generals and politicians and office seekers to the infirm, the destitute, and the ordinary. By revealing Lincoln through the observations of others and relating him to almost everything that happened in his shell-torn land, Sandburg is trying to sketch a portrait "both of the Lincoln who belonged to the people and the people who belonged to Lincoln," as North Callahan has written.

So, in these "tornado years" of war, Lincoln is still the people's hero. He is the umpire of an embattled Union, patiently sticking to the cherished middle way. His "skilled referee hand" guides the ship of state through cross winds of passion and cross plays of hate, until at last he has controlled the storm. Throughout he has the folk masses behind him. He is still their Friendly Stranger in a maelstrom of chaos and death. Even during his lowest ebb in

1864, Sandburg's Lincoln remains the people's president; he retains their love and loyalty even as Republican leaders raise a howl against his renomination and reelection. And he wins in 1864 because the will of the people prevails.

Moreover, in the last long year of the war, Sandburg's Lincoln does battle with the so-called radicals of the party—vengeful cynics like Charles Sumner and Thaddeus Stevens who want to exterminate the South's ruling class and convert Dixie into "a vast graveyard of slaughtered whites, with Negro State governments established and upheld by Northern white bayonets." But a mild and moderate Lincoln refuses to go along with them. He is now in his grandest hour, this Lincoln of the *War Years*, as he plans to reconstruct the South with tenderness and magnanimity. He is the only man in the entire country who can peaceably reunite the sections. But as in a Greek tragedy, Lincoln is murdered before he can bind up the nation's wounds and heal the antagonisms of his divided countrymen. In North and South, common people weep aloud, realizing the painful truth of the old folk adage that a tree is measured best when it is down. "Silence, grief, and quiet resolves," Sandburg writes, "these only were left for those who admired and loved and felt themselves close to a living presence that was one of them."

In evaluating the *War Years* as biography, one must give Sandburg the accolades he is due. For all four volumes are superior examples of artistic narration. In truth, Sandburg's literary powers are on grand display now: here clearly is a master storyteller, spicing his narrative with lively vignettes, heightening tension by postponing lines of action, closing chapters with quotations that foreshadow great and ominous events. The *War Years* are filled with climaxes and lulls, with rises and falls, with the very heartbeat of fine literature. And in the chapter on the Gettysburg Address, Sandburg allows himself a burst of poetic imagery as moving as anything I have ever read.

Nevertheless, from the view of true biography, the *War Years* like the earlier volumes are marred by a plethora of apocryphal stories and unauthenticated scenes. A good example is the episode where a sad and humble Lincoln visits the Joint Committee on the Conduct of the War and defends Mary Lincoln's loyalty in a solemn testimony. Like so many of Sandburg's stories, this one cannot be substantiated by convincing evidence and doubtlessly never happened. The trouble is that Sandburg draws uncritically and at length from the writings of almost everybody who ever saw or heard or claimed to know something about the president. He quotes from reliable witnesses like John Hay and Gideon Welles, but he also takes information from highly unreliable ones like Count Gurowski and the anonymous Public Man, whose diary is part fact and part fantasy. As a consequence, the *War Years* are a perplexing mélange of authentic eyewitness accounts, hearsay, lore and legend. But untutored readers, alas, tend to embrace everything in the book as fact.

Worse still, from the view of biographical truth, is Sandburg's legend-building portrait of Lincoln himself. First of all, it is difficult to see how Lincoln could remain a folk hero throughout the war, when in fact he was the most unpopular president the Republic had known up to that time. His hate mail from the public was voluminous and grotesque, as for instance the letter awaiting him in Washington in February 1861: "You are nothing but a goddamn Black nigger." Moreover, it is simply not true to assert (as Sandburg does) that Lincoln "knew his American people" when it came to emancipation and acted always in accordance with their wishes. On the contrary, Lincoln was far ahead of public opinion when he issued the Emancipation Proclamation, as evidenced by the massive racist backlash it ignited among Union voters—common and upper class alike—who feared it would bring Southern blacks stampeding into Northern neighborhoods. To ward off political disaster, Lincoln and his party worked hard to sell Northern whites on the necessity for slave liberation—and to assuage their racial fears. But as I've said, emancipation remained the most unpopular act of Lincoln's beleaguered administration.

Furthermore, it is impossible to accept Sandburg's contention that, in the dark and dismal days of 1864, Lincoln continued to enjoy the unswerving loyalty of the people. How can this be when Lincoln himself and most Republican campaigners were convinced that he was too controversial and hated to be reelected? When he *was* reelected, he owed his triumph, not to the adoration of the folk masses, but to Sherman's capture of Atlanta, to Lincoln's own adroit dealings with dissident members of his party, and to the folly of the Democrats in running a major general on a peace platform in the midst of Civil War. Sumner was close to the truth when he remarked that the election was a "vote *against*

McClellan rather than *for* Lincoln." And if I may digress, it is difficult to embrace the Lincoln of the Civil War as a national folk hero, a president of the people, when he never commanded the huge popular majorities that later swept Lyndon Baines Johnson and Richard M. Nixon into the White House. If we persist in regarding an unpopular Lincoln as a hero of the masses, should not Johnson and Nixon qualify as *super* folk heroes, even more beloved of the people than the Civil War president?

There are other problems with Sandburg's *War Years*. For one thing, he scarcely does justice to Lincoln's evolving emancipation policy. In truth, he glosses over the complex, step-by-step journey Lincoln took to his Proclamation. When difficult decisions must be made about slavery, Sandburg almost always has Lincoln telling stories. He does not mention Lincoln's carriage ride with Seward and Gideon Welles, in July 1862, when the president spoke urgently and forcefully about hurling his armies against slavery in the rebel South and making whites there pay the price of civil war. Moreover, Sandburg does not explain the crucial difference between Lincoln's Proclamation and the second confiscation act, does not observe that Lincoln's decree was a declaration of war not only against the institution of slavery in the rebellious states, but against the South's master class whose very existence depended on human bondage. Sandburg may have had good reason to leave this and the carriage ride out of his story: both would undermine his image of Lincoln as a moderate and gentle man in his treatment of Southern rebels.

In that regard, it is manifestly inaccurate to argue (as Sandburg does) that Lincoln clung to the middle of the road throughout the war, constantly moderating between opposing extremes, constantly playing off so-called radicals and conservatives against one another as he held his middle course. In point of fact, Lincoln was always closest to Sumner's wing of the party. Not only did the president regard Sumner and his colleagues as the conscience of the party; he also told Sumner in December 1861 that in the matter of emancipation he was only a month to six weeks behind the senator. And that proved pretty much the case. Moreover, as the conflict ground on with no end in sight, Lincoln embraced almost every harsh measure the so-called radicals urged on him— not only emancipation, but confiscation, conscription, and the use of Negro troops. As a consequence, conservative Republicans and dissident Democrats wailed in despair, complaining that Lincoln was a tool of the abolitionists—or that he himself was an abolitionist and a dictator to boot.

When it came to reconstruction, moreover, Lincoln did not play some forgiving middle role, while Sumner and his fellow "extremists" conspired to carve Dixie up in an ecstasy of revenge. In actuality, Lincoln and Sumner stood together on a number of reconstruction issues. Both agreed that the South had to be remade. Both wanted to vanquish slavery forever. Both wanted to muzzle the rebellious white majority in Dixie, lest it overwhelm the Unionists there and return the old Southern ruling class to power. Far from forgiving that class (as Sandburg suggests), Lincoln agreed with Sumner that it should be eradicated, and the president's emancipation and reconstruction policies were calculated to do precisely that.

Where Sumner and Lincoln clashed, of course, was over which branch of the government—the Congress or the presidency— should administer reconstruction and remake the conquered South. And they also disagreed over the role of the army in the reconstruction process. But it was Sumner—not Lincoln—who opposed military reconstruction during the war, contending that "the eggs of crocodiles can produce only crocodiles, and it is not easy to see how eggs laid by military power can be hatched into an American state." By contrast, as I have pointed out, it was Lincoln who emphatically endorsed military reconstruction. Yet Sandburg nowhere makes this clear. Nor does he explain that, in their last cabinet meeting, Lincoln and all his Secretaries thought an army of occupation might well be necessary to reconstruct the South. In other words, the president was already considering in 1865 what Congress would finally adopt two years later.

One could go on, but the point is that Sandburg's *War Years,* like his *Prairie Years,* cannot be regarded as authentic biography, as a careful and accurate approximation of the real-life Lincoln. Does this mean, then, that the work has no value, that it must be kept from the eyes of impressionable students? No, it does not mean that at all. For if not true to biographical art, Sandburg's volumes *are* true to mythical art. And it is imperative that students and all other readers understand the difference, understand that what Sandburg has really given us is a true and powerful rendering of our most celebrated mythical hero. In that respect,

Sandburg's *Lincoln* is reminiscent of a Wagnerian musical drama, of *Tristan Und Isolde*, the *Entrance of the Gods into Valhalla*, or the *Preludes to Lohengrin*. Like them, Sandburg's volumes roll and thunder, whisper and cry, with all the grandeur of a historic and indigenous mythology. Again, Sandburg himself was aware of the musical passion that drove his story; and this passion came from his mythic vision of his subject—of a "baffling and completely inexplicable" Lincoln who embodied the mystical genius of America's folk masses. In truth, the Lincoln portrayed in Sandburg's lyrical narrative possesses what Americans have always considered their most noble traits—honesty, unpretentiousness, tolerance, hard work, a capacity to forgive, a compassion for the underdog, a clear-sighted vision of what is right and what is wrong, a dedication to God and country, and an abiding concern for all. No real-life person has ever risen to such mythic proportions, to epitomize all that we have longed to be since 1776. No real-life person can ever rise to such proportions. So we have invented a Lincoln who fulfills our deepest needs as a people—a Father Abraham who in the stormy present still provides an example and shows us the way. The Lincoln of mythology carries the torch of the American dream, a dream of noble idealism, of self-sacrifice and common humanity, of liberty and equality for all.

Our folly as a nation, though, is that we too often confuse myth with history, mistake our mythologized heroes for their real-life counterparts, regard the deified Washington as the actual Washington. As a consequence, we too often try to emulate our mythical leaders, to be as glorious, as powerful, as incapable of error, as incessantly right, as we have made them. By contrast, traditional myth-bound cultures have understood the difference between myth and reality, folk gods and actual human beings. An ancient Greek would have laughed out loud had somebody told him that Orpheus was a real man. A myth was not about real people. It was an inspiring story about legendary figures; it revealed a great deal about the needs of one's culture; it helped in one's own self-discovery. If we Americans can follow the example of traditional myth-bound societies, if we can accept our myths as inspiring tales rather than as authentic biography and history, then perhaps myths can serve us, too. Like fiction and poetry, they can give us insight into ourselves, help us understand the spiritual longings of our country, as we cope with the complex realities of our own time. In that event, the Lincoln of mythology—the Plain and Humble Man of the People who emerged from the toiling millions to guide us steadily through our greatest national ordeal —can have profound spiritual meaning for us. And no one has captured that Lincoln with such poetry and deep music as Carl Sandburg.

NINE

GHOST RIDERS IN THE SKY

H E who invokes history is al-
ways secure," Czeslaw Milosz once observed, for "the dead will
not rise to witness against him." In our time, a number of American politicians, activists, and commentators have invoked the
history of the frontier and the immutable "lessons" it furnishes
us today. One can find plenty of lyrical references to the frontier
—and the romantic, two-fisted heroes who conquered it—in Paul
Harvey's radio newscasts, in John Wayne's public utterances and
his remarkable interview in *Playboy Magazine*, and in the
speeches and writings of western Republicans like Ronald Reagan. In their individual ways, these self-styled conservatives
dredge up the "lessons" of the Old West not only to justify their
political philosophy, but to vindicate their crusade against liberal
"do-gooders" and paternalistic government. In truth, all of them
view Big Government as one of the chief villains in the modern-
American scenario, and all are out to gun down what they regard
as Big Government's most contemptible offspring: Welfare, Civil
Rights, and Business Regulation. These, the conservatives contend, have done much to destroy those immortal freedoms our
frontier forefathers passed on to us—initiative, rugged individualism, and free enterprise—and to surrender the United States
to Communism. In his radio histrionics, Chicago's Paul Harvey
blasts away at all signs of socialism in the United States and lectures his fellow Americans for selling out their glorious pioneer
heritage. Ronald Reagan, for his part, charges that the liberals, in
their "remote and massive strong-arming from afar," are out to
obliterate "the unique powers of the individual and his personal

opinions." All the liberals want, Reagan warns, is a bureaucratic dictatorship and "the submergence of man in statistics."

For Reagan and his compatriots, all this means war. And while "the guns are silent in this war," he and his men are determined that no more "frontiers" will fall to American leftists, that under Reagan's banners (*Down with Welfare Government, Restore Free Enterprise*) individual freedom will yet survive on these shores.

John Wayne emphatically agrees. He contends that our frontier experience teaches us above all that Americans have got to make it on their own, have got to reject government handouts for sitting on their backsides. And that includes Negroes and Indians. "We'll all be on a reservation soon if the socialists keep subsidizing groups like them with our tax money," Wayne told *Playboy Magazine*. But while welfare is anti-American enough, the worst menace to the American way of life are the Communists right here in the United States who distribute propaganda that belittles "our great country" and her heroes. Echoing Harvey, Reagan, and other American patriots, Wayne blames the liberals for the Communist conspiracy "within our borders." It began, he insists, with Franklin Roosevelt "who gave the world Communism" and it has grown in modern times, when liberals have allowed "known Communists" to teach in American schools, have allowed instructors (in the words of a Los Angeles news columnist) to "pervert the natural loyalties and ideals of our kids, filling them with fear and doubt and hate and downgrading patriotism and all our heroes of the past."

In Wayne's mind, America's greatest heroes were the powerful he-men of Western mythology, who pulverized Indians and rustlers alike and who took no lip from anybody. While he concedes that these legendary frontiersmen might have made some mistakes, he defends what they did to the Indians. "Our so-called stealing of this country from them was just a matter of survival," he explained to *Playboy*. "There were great numbers of people who needed new land, and the Indians were selfishly trying to keep it for themselves." Of course, Wayne would not grant Communist China the right to seize southeast Asia on the same principle. On the contrary, he advocated all-out war with the Communists there, insisting that the United States ought to move in with atomic bombs and clean the Reds out of Indochina "with dispatch." He solemnly warned that to smash the Communists both overseas and here at home, Americans must be iron-fisted and mean-eyed, like the cowboys Wayne has played in most of his Westerns.

Wayne's fast-action Western's (like Ronald Reagan's, Tom Mix's, and Hopalong Cassidy's) are veritable respositories of Old West mythology—the cinematic descendants of Erastus Beadle's chimerical dime novels of a century ago. Like those legend-building novels, Wayne's movies have been enormously popular in the United States, especially among those who have little interest in nuances and complexities and who like to solve problems through physical confrontation. Of the legion of Wayne admirers, perhaps the most celebrated is Richard M. Nixon, who, on one notable occasion during his presidency, expatiated not only on frontier justice but on the immense appeal of Wayne-style Westerns. It was August 3, 1970, and Nixon was addressing a group of reporters in Denver, Colorado, the site of a federal-state law enforcement conference the president was attending. As Nixon explained it, he was in San Clemente during the past weekend and enjoyed a special presidential viewing of *Chisum,* a new John Wayne film about the Lincoln County cattle war in the old New Mexico Territory. Wildly inaccurate in its portrayal of actual historical figures and events, the movie defended Billy the Kid as basically a good sort, a Bible-reading youth who took to killing bad people out of revenge for a murdered benefactor. But the real hero was John Wayne in the title role as Chisum. A strong, single, hardworking cowman, Chisum discovers that the Lincoln County establishment is corrupt to the core, that the sheriff and his deputies are all hired guns for Lawrence Murphy, a crooked, power-grabbing cattle king. Finally, Chisum does the only thing a good man can do: he takes the law into his own hands and with his cowboys (Pat Garrett and Billy the Kid among them) smashes the lowdown Murphy gang in an old-fashioned shoot-out. Thanks to Chisum, Garrett becomes the new sheriff and justice triumphs in Lincoln County.

Nixon was entranced. "As I looked at that movie," he told reporters in Denver, "I said, 'Well, it was a very good Western. John Wayne is a fine actor and it had a fine supporting cast.' " After the movie, Nixon got to wondering why the Western had retained its tremendous popularity over the years. One reason, to be sure, was all "the gun play." But the major reason, Nixon decided, was that Westerns "conveyed a simple but enduring moral message: 'The good guys come out ahead in the Westerns; the bad guys lose.' "

Westerns like *Chisum* demonstrated something else, too. "In the end, as this movie particularly pointed out, even in the old West, before New Mexico was a state, there was a time when there was no law. But the law eventually came, and the law was important from the standpoint of not only prosecuting the guilty but also seeing that those who were guilty had a proper trial."

As it went in John Wayne's Westerns, so it had gone in America's proud and unprecedented history. In Nixon's view, Americans so far had always come out on top (had never lost a war, had made theirs the mightiest nation on earth) because they had been the good guys, their enemies the bad guys. Why had Americans been the good guys? Because up to now they had always had an abiding respect for law and order. Because they had always demonstrated unimpeachable moral rectitude, two-fisted physical supremacy, and an inflexible will to win.

But in Nixon's opinion too many young Americans today no longer cared about the law or about moral and military superiority. This, too, he thought about after seeing *Chisum*. And this he told reporters in Denver. Why had American young people lost their respect for the law? Nixon meant no criticism, but he attributed part of the problem to the news media, which tended to glorify dissenters and crooks . . . like Charles Manson, for example, whose trial for the Sharon Tate murders was under way in California at the same time that Nixon was speaking in Denver. Yes, the president said, he was concerned about the Manson case, because the media had sensationalized the event, presenting Manson himself as a "rather glamorous figure." Yet in reality, Nixon declared, Manson "was guilty, either directly or indirectly, of eight murders without reason."

After what he had said about frontier justice and respect for the law, this was an incredible remark, for the president of the United States—a professional lawyer—had pronounced Manson guilty before the court had found him so, something that could have prejudiced the outcome of the trial. The news media criticized Nixon so sharply that he later retracted the statement about Manson. But the president stuck to his guns about the moral lesson inherent in what he said about Western movies and respect for law and order. It was high time for young people to stand up for America and to stop praising "those who deliberately disrupt."

On numerous other occasions, Nixon beseeched his country-men to live by the lessons of the past—lessons he learned from his own study of history, which began when his Aunt Edith gave him an American history text for his tenth birthday, and which continued when he became a star history student at California's Whittier College.* Not surprisingly, Nixon's "lessons" from the past were almost identical to the frontier virtues trumpeted in Harvey's newcasts, Reagan's speeches, and Wayne's cowboy movies, not to mention all the chauvinistic histories and hero-worshipping biographies (of Daniel Boone and Davy Crockett, of Wyatt Earp and Kit Carson) that grace our schools and libraries. Here are some of Nixon's lessons:

On the strength and the will to win: "History is full of examples of civilizations with superior ideas which have gone down to defeat because their adversaries had more will to win, more raw strength physically, mentally, and emotionally, to throw into the critical battles."

On physical superiority: "America will not tolerate being pushed around by anybody." "Little men with great fears are always ready to cry in anguish that a strong policy risks war. History proves that they are wrong and dangerously wrong." "The lesson of all history warns us that we should negotiate only when our military supremacy is so convincing that we can achieve our objective at the conference table—and deny the aggressor his."

On rugged individualism (The national lesson): "America became a great country because for 190 years we have proceeded on a great principle. America became great not because of what government did for people but because of what people did for themselves." (The personal lesson): *"The ability to be cool, confident, and decisive in crisis is not an inherited characteristic but is the direct result of how well the individual has prepared himself for battle."*

On good confronting evil (with reference to John Foster Dulles):

---

* As a history student at Whittier, recalled one of Nixon's professors, "Dick had the uncommon capacity to brush aside the façades of a subject and get at the heart of it. He always completed in half a page what would take a normal 'A' student two pages." See Earl Mazo and Stephen Hess, *Nixon, A Political Portrait* (New York, 1967), 19.

"He had a vision of the world that placed the daily swirl of events in the context of history. In the global clash between the free world and the totalitarian communist bloc, Dulles believed that he had found as close an approximation of the struggle between good and evil as one is likely to find in this imperfect world. . . . History will record the 'inflexibility' and 'brinkmanship' for which Dulles was criticized in truth represented basic principles of the highest order."

With such convictions as these, it was no wonder that Nixon applauded the swift, simplistic, tough-guy approach to victory and justice portrayed in Westerns like *Chisum*. And it was no wonder that as president Nixon identified himself as the leader of the good guys and looked on almost everybody who disagreed with him—newsmen, northeastern Republicans, liberal Democrats, and protesting students and intellectuals—as mortal enemies of the president and therefore of rightness itself. For Nixon and his men, domestic politics became a desperate battleground between *them* and *us*, between the forces of evil and the forces of good, between a gang of traitors and an administration of patriots who alone could save this Republic. In the name of the Republic, the Nixon forces took the law into their own hands (as Chisum and his cowboys had done): they compiled an "enemies list," used the Internal Revenue Service to harass political opponents, wire-tapped government officials and private citizens, established an elaborate spy system inside the White House, collected hundreds of thousands of dollars in illegal campaign contributions, hired thugs to ransack the psychiatric files of antiwar dissident Daniel Ellsberg, authorized the burglary of Democratic national headquarters at the Watergate complex in Washington, D.C., and then tried to cover up the burglary through pay-offs, lies, and a systematic obstruction of justice. The climax came in a series of high-noon shoot-outs between Nixon and gangs of special prosecutors and meddling congressmen—except that the ending in Nixon's scenario turned out differently from that in *Chisum*. For at the conclusion of Watergate, Nixon stood stripped of his cloak of moral and historical righteousness and faced the cameras for what he really was: a vengeful California politician who, like the frontier speculator of old, had no morality at all.

Nevertheless, there are millions of Americans who still regard Nixon as a hero and who share the Nixon-Wayne-Reagan view of the Old West, a myth-ridden view that celebrates power, manly confrontations, and black-and-white moralities. But in spite of its widespread popularity, their view doesn't have much to do with historical reality, any more than it provides valid lessons for getting along in the real world. To begin with, it ought to be obvious that the real world is a lot more complex than the simplistic conflicts and easy solutions of Western mythology. To emulate the two-fisted cowboy and his love of direct action will not work for a nation whose problems, as Joe B. Frantz put it, "are corporate, community, and complex." Moreover, the real frontier itself was far more complicated than the playlike West portrayed in the formula Westerns—movies in which the good guys "came out ahead" primarily because they were white, Protestant, tight-lipped, and tough. The bad guys were either Indians, Mexicans, or lubricious, sissified white misfits who hated to work.

As far as frontier justice goes, even Wayne ought to know that vigilante hangings occurred all over the West—even after there were sheriffs and established courts—and that those who did the lynching generally thought they were right. They were the good guys. Sometimes their victims were suspected rustlers; at other times they were ornery dissidents, suspicious-looking Mexicans, Chinese coolies, or Indian "niggers" accused of messing around with white women. And vigilante terrorism in the name of right and morality was still going on in the 1920s, in the turbulent oil-boom towns in Texas and Oklahoma. Furthermore, not all men who succeeded in the real West were good guys in any sense, for among them were parasitic speculators, political opportunists, effete swindlers, and racist cavalrymen who enjoyed killing Indians—women and children included—because, as General Philip Sheridan argued, "the only good Indian is a dead one."

Moreover, the contention that American frontiersmen were rugged he-men who did everything for themselves, who never received aid from the government or assistance from their neighbors, is absurd. While there is no denying the courage and self-reliance a great many pioneers displayed in settling the West, they were nevertheless uninhibited nationalists who looked to Washington for free land, military protection, favorable tariff and monetary policies, government-subsidized railroads, and political machinery for their territorial and state governments. In fact, the cattle barons—those examples of supreme rugged individualism—

enjoyed a tremendous federal subsidy in the form of free range on government land. But what a howl they raised when Washington moved to legalize individual homesteads there. Finally, in the early 1890s Western farmers and small businessmen helped found the Populist party, a people's movement designed to win the federal government away from Eastern industrial and political interests and to correct the worst inequities of unbridled capitalism.

Nor did all pioneers rely on brute strength—on military superiority—to defend their freedom or to solve their problems. While six-gun violence was commonplace on the frontier, many settlers found that a healthy cooperative spirit, imbued with mutual trust and understanding, resolved conflicts that guns and muscle only exacerbated. The Mormons, for their part, employed rugged collectivism to survive in the sun-blistered Utah desert. And out on the windy plains homestead families depended on one another in a variety of ways. They not only banded together against claim-jumpers, marauding cattlemen, and retaliating Indians, but also helped each other build their farms, plant and harvest crops, and manage through births and deaths. It was a rare family that survived on the prairies without the help of neighbors. There are also examples of how preachers, school teachers, lawyers, and other unarmed respectables tamed Wild West towns, not with fists and pistols, but with sheer determination to lock up the cowboys' guns, stop the brawls and shoot-outs, and teach people something about respect for their neighbors and for dissenting points of view. So the lessons of the frontier do not always prove that for freedom and law and order to triumph, Americans have got to outshoot and outfight everybody in sight.

Still, I doubt that such observations will intrigue John Wayne, Ronald Reagan, Paul Harvey, former President Nixon, and all their followers. For these men are not much interested in historical reality. For them, history is useful only if it can serve their political needs, only if it can provide slogans and symbols that justify their views and mobilize support for their crusade against liberals, dissidents, socialists, Communists, and Democrats.

This is not to say that men like Wayne and Reagan are hypocrites. On the contrary, they sincerely believe that their romantic version of Western history is true, that America's birth and westward expansion were divinely ordained, that the ideal Americans are still the rugged individualists of Western mythology, and that only this mythology, with its right-against-wrong simplicities, can supply the strength and virtue America needs to overcome her present enemies—the Reds of our time.

Nor are conservative Republicans the only advocates who abuse history for political ends. Politicians of all ideologies and all nations do it with unblushing sincerity every day. Still, while one can understand the role of historical myth in man's struggle for local, national, and world dominion, let us recall what is sacrificed when history is no longer viewed as a source of enlightenment, when it serves only to vindicate some party line. Then the living truths of the past—what previous generations have learned as they struggled with universal human dilemmas—are lost forever in a morass of historical and political moralizing.

TEN

THEMES AND VARIATIONS OF A
CIVIL WAR TRILOGY

I

W HEN I began graduate studies in history in 1958, I was fascinated by the polygonal nature of the discipline. One could, I discovered, approach the past from any number of perspectives: as a social scientist who studies forces and trends; as a quantifier who employs statistics to illuminate patterns of behavior; as an intellectualist who explores the role and impact of ideas; or as a humanist who focuses on the human side of the past, examining how the interaction of people and events shaped the course of history.

Almost from the start, I was drawn to the humanistic approach, which made me something of a maverick even in graduate school. For in the late 1950s professional historians as a group were moving away from humanistic history, and in the next twenty years would function increasingly as sociologists and statisticians, pouring their research into recondite, technical studies written largely for one another. During those years, I traveled a different road from most of my peers, a road that took me back to historical writing as literature—an old and honorable tradition too often disparaged in our analytical time. Inevitably, I was attracted to biography as the form in which I wanted to write about the past, because true biography—the best biography—was an art that brought people alive again, calling up and sharing "the warmth of a life being lived," as the late Paul Murray Kendall expressed it. As I studied biography and historical narration, relishing the works of William Hickling Prescott, Lytton Strachey, André Maurois, Garrett Mattingly, Paul Horgan, Wallace Stegner, the younger Arthur Schlesinger Jr., and Kendall himself, I admired the way they transported me back into the past, giving me the sense of being there with the people they described. I also admired their literary techniques—their use of metaphor and time, their symphonic organization, and above all their development of character. I reveled in the fact that artful biography was not abstract, was not an analysis of lifeless data and impersonal force, was not an academic lecture in which the author pompously upstages his own subject (the problem with almost all academic and "critical" biographies), but was a form of literature like fiction. Unlike the novelist, as I have said, the biographer is limited to what actually happened and cannot invent situations and make up dialogue. But like the novelist, the true biographer must have an eye for detail and must learn the technique of controlled dramatic narration; he must keep his own voice out of the story so that the subject and his times can live again; and he must have insight into character, know how to depict complex interpersonal relationships, capture the inexplicable, and rely on the power of suggestion—especially through the telling quotation. At the same time, the true biographer must have a professional mastery of the era in which his subject lived and died, which requires exhaustive, painstaking research in all the pertinent archival and printed sources. In sum, the true biographer must be both an historian who is steeped in his material and an artist who wields a deft and vivid pen.

Because of my love for literature, I found biography a tremendous challenge and eventually committed myself to the form, to trying to understand the past through the particular lives of individuals. In the process, I hoped to learn something about human nature itself and the universal truths held in common by people of all generations and all societies.

After several experimental efforts, I conceived a biographical trilogy on the greater Civil War era, a trilogy that might illuminate that apocalyptic era through the intersecting lives of three central figures—the slave rebel Nat Turner, the abolitionist John Brown, and the Republican President Abraham Lincoln. All three were inextricably caught up in the slavery issue of their day and all devised their own solutions to that monstrous and inflammable problem. And they all died, too, in the conflicts and hostilities that slavery generated.

Nat Turner, for his part, was the victim of human bondage, a brilliant slave preacher prevented from ever achieving his full potential. Nat's slave life was a prison of sorrow and frustration, a living jail in which he anguished over his condition and that of his people and longed for freedom all the more because he knew he couldn't have it. He was indeed like a powerful angel with his wings nailed to the ground. And he suffered for another reason, too, for his wife and children were enslaved on another farm in backwater Southampton County, down in southeastern Virginia. So Nat was doomed to live apart from his family, an absentee husband and father who worked and slept alone on his master's farm. At last, too intelligent and frustrated to remain somebody's property, aroused to a biblical rage by his own religious fantasies and the emotional revivalism of the time, Nat rose up against the slave system like a furious biblical prophet, thundering that Jehovah had appointed him an instrument of divine vengeance to free his people and punish guilty whites. As Nat interpreted his holy mission, he was to reconstruct his world along revolutionary lines, creating a new order in which "the first should be last and the last should be first." And so out of Nat's secular frustrations and religious visions came the winds of his fierce rebellion, a storm of black rage that swept across Southampton County and consumed more than 220 lives including Nat's own. In *The Fires of Jubilee*, I tried to narrate Nat's story as graphically and accurately as I could. I wanted readers to suffer with Nat and see the world of slavery and the Old South through his eyes. That way they might gain melancholy insight into what it was like to be a slave. Moreover, by placing Nat and his revolt in proper historical context, I hoped to convey how the insurrection rocked the South to its foundations and pointed the way to civil war thirty years later.

In contrast to Nat Turner, John Brown was a white Northerner who hated slavery from the outside. I have explained in other chapters why he loathed bondage so. But I haven't indicated how slavery in America imperiled Brown himself and his family. Brown had striven hard to endure his trial on earth and prepare himself for paradise and a union with his Calvinist God. Yet that same God, in a burst of omniscient rage, might well destroy

Brown's slave-cursed land and sweep all Americans—Brown and his wife and children included—into the fires of an everlasting hell. As Brown smoldered over the manifold evils of slavery, he also suffered through a failure-scarred life that in itself reveals a lot about human suffering. And it reveals a great deal about nineteenth-century America, too, since Brown struggled for forty years to succeed in the system as a Christian businessman, only to fail again and again. In the end, as I have shown, Brown abandoned the American system and became a revolutionary like Nat Turner, attacking slavery from the outside in hopes of setting off a chain of Turner-style rebellions. In Southern eyes, of course, Brown was Nat Turner reincarnated, a Yankee abolitionist sent by the "Black" Republican party to drown the South in rivers of blood. Because Harpers Ferry linked Southern fears of revolt and insurrection with Southern fears of the Republican party, Brown, too, was enormously significant in the rush of irreversible events that bore the United States toward civil war.

By comparison, Abraham Lincoln shunned violence and revolution and worked all his life inside the American system, elevating himself from an Indiana farm boy to a literate and successful lawyer and finally to the highest political office in the land. Lincoln loved America and extolled her example and promise in the world with more clarity and eloquence than anyone of his generation, maybe of any generation. But the fact that he personally hated slavery as much as John Brown did left Lincoln trapped in an impossible dilemma. He detested slavery and yet revered a political system which protected that very institution. True, Lincoln tried to convince himself that if contained in the South, human bondage would die out some day and the Republic would at last right itself with its noblest ideals. But slavery continued to make Lincoln miserable, for it prevented black people from elevating themselves as he had done and violated his sense of decency and fair play. Lincoln's dilemma—his hatred of slavery and his impotence to do anything about it where it already existed—undoubtedly fed his melancholy like wind on flames.

One of the supreme ironies of Lincoln's life—and of my trilogy —was that he who spurned violence, he who placed his reverence for the system above his loathing of slavery, ended up smashing the institution in a violent civil war, a war that began because Southerners equated Lincoln with John Brown and Nat Turner and seceded from the very system that protected slavery from Lincoln's grasp. To save the American system, Lincoln finally liberated the slaves. And in the process he freed himself from his dilemma. For emancipation brought the private and the public Lincoln together: the public statesman could now obliterate what the private citizen had always detested. Then when both sides— the North and the South, Lincoln and the slaveowner—had paid for their complicity in the crime of human bondage, they could bind up their wounds and "do all which may achieve and cherish a just, and a lasting peace," as Lincoln proclaimed in his second Inaugural Address. Some six weeks later, fuming at Lincoln for emancipating the "niggers" and blaming him for all the country's woes, John Wilkes Booth murdered the president at Ford's Theater, certain that assassination would make him a national hero. Like Brown, Lincoln went on to martyrdom and legend, inflated by the myth-makers into a godly Emancipator who personified America's ideal Everyman.

So my biographies of Turner, Brown, and Lincoln intersect at several levels—as their lives intersected—and demonstrate how all three were profoundly influential in the outbreak of civil war and the final destruction of slavery in their troubled and paradoxical land. At the same time, each biography can be read strictly on its own merits, for each is about a unique human being whose value, as Lytton Strachey would say, "is independent of any temporal process" and can be appreciated "for its own sake."

II

Because it must make the people of history live and sing again, true biography must be more than the sum of one's research notes —more than the presentation of what one has gleaned from letters, journals, diaries, reminiscences, and other contemporary accounts. The prose of the true biographer must radiate a sense of intimacy and familiarity, quite as though the author himself has lived the life and walked the ground. And this is a quality that can only be acquired by visiting the landmarks where one's subject lived and died. In the course of writing about John Brown, I journeyed across eastern Kansas where the civil war of 1856 had flamed, taking notes on the landscape, the murderous thunderstorms, and the howling winds that lashed the area where Brown's Station was located, and comparing these to descriptions recorded in Brown's time. As I stood rooted to the spot, the sounds of Bleeding Kansas—of artillery salvos, pounding hooves, shouts and gunfire—echoed in the windy trees around me. And I could almost see Brown and his guerrilla band as they rode across the prairie there to ransack proslavery homesteads and fight proslavery men. Later I visited the John Brown farm in the Adirondack Mountains of upstate New York. I stood at the front of Brown's cabin and stared at the frozen grandeur of the mountains, sensing the solitude as Brown sensed it. No wonder the old man felt at home in the Adirondacks. Up here in the mountains, as though suspended between Heaven and Earth, he could feel closer to his God.

In my search for Brown, I also visited Harpers Ferry, nestled in the Blue Ridge Mountains, at the confluence of the Shenandoah and Potomac rivers, and looking much as it did in Brown's time. With my notes and maps, I re-enacted the entire raid, moving down from the Maryland mountains and descending on Harpers Ferry just as Brown and his men had done that drizzly October night in 1859. I could almost hear the shouts and gunshots that rang over the town after Brown had captured the arsenal there, could see two of Brown's men getting cut down in a cross fire in the Shenandoah, could see Brown himself fighting desperately to hold the fire-engine house from Robert E. Lee's horse marines. . . .

Like my visits to Kansas and upstate New York, my journey to Harpers Ferry made Brown come alive for me. And in the act of writing *To Purge This Land with Blood,* I became utterly and completely immersed in his life and times. I dreamed about him and the Kansas civil war and Harpers Ferry, and once had a mild hallucination, catching a glimpse of the old man in the doorway of my study, his steel-gray eyes fixed on me as I typed his story. Yes, he lived again in my mind, so much so that after the book was done and off in the mails, I lay around for days, lost in his world, beset with images of Harpers Ferry and Brown's trial and hanging.

The same thing happened with Nat Turner. My wife Ruth and I went to Southampton County and retraced the entire rebellion, in what turned out to be one of the most memorable experiences of my life. In truth, being on the ground gave me a feel for Nat— a sense of the land he lived in, its forests, sounds, smells, and its people both black and white—I could have secured in no other way. Also, many of the homes that figured in the revolt still stand today, haunted gray relics of time. I walked around and stood inside those old cobwebbed museums, hearing the cries and terrible sounds that reverberated through them when the slave insurgents attacked. Visiting the old homes carried me back to Nat's time, back to the rebellion he led, so that when I stood in a shack where Nat's wife and children may have lived, I was stricken with the revelation that 1831 was only yesterday.

When I wrote the Nat Turner book, I included an epilogue about my journey to Southampton County, trying to demonstrate that a good deal more goes into true biography than reading documents and books in a library. Also, the epilogue had an artistic purpose, for I wanted to show that past and present are indeed a continuum. In fact, the last scene of the epilogue circled back thematically to 1832 and revealed a sad truth about the durability of human prejudice. In 1832, a Virginia newspaper editor, in defending gradual emancipation and colonization over immediate manumission, argued that whites could not overcome their racial hostilities overnight. In the epilogue, I quoted a Virginia banker who said the same thing in 1973.

As with John Brown, Nat Turner lingered on in my mind long after I had completed *The Fires of Jubilee*, as though his experiences—his life and death—were somehow my own. Unable to shake off thoughts of Nat, I sat one night in a dark and smoky lounge in Amherst, listening to a black musician play jazz on his trumpet and making all manner of connections with the slave music of Nat's world. Presently the musician launched into an old blues song, and its mournful refrains sent me spiraling irretrievably back to Southampton County of 1831. With my eyes closed now and the trumpet sounding sadly in the distance, I was with Nat as he ran desperately through Southampton County, trying to elude the white patrols out to get him with their dogs. I cried, "Run, Nat! For Christ's sake, run," as he crashed through the very forests and fields I had visited, until at last he hid himself under a pile of fence rails. With dogs howling in the distance, I stared at his face—a lined, contorted face—and was stunned by the depth of his suffering. Then the scene changed, and Nat was struggling along the road to Jerusalem, escorted by an armed guard through a sea of hostile whites. . . . Then he was standing under the hanging tree, a chorus swelling across the horizon as he prepared fiercely and silently to die. . . . And for an eternal moment, as the trumpet wailed from across a universe of time, I felt I wouldn't make it back from Nat's world, felt that I too was doomed there, menaced by some unseen and unutterable violence about to descend on me like an invisible guillotine. . . . But then I felt my wife's hand on my arm and opened my eyes in the gloomy Amherst lounge. The trumpet player was sitting down at our table. Ah, Alden, how good to see you. You play a mean trumpet, man. Meaner than you know.

When I turned to Lincoln and set out in search of him, I ran into difficulties. For one thing, his house in Springfield—an impressive two-story structure that befitted his professional and social status—is a popular historical site, clogged with sightseers come to pay homage to the legend. I was swept along in a bustling line of visitors, trying hard to envision Lincoln in his rocking chair there in the living room, lost in one of his abstractions for which he became famous. I went to his law office across from the state capitol, imagining him sprawled across the old sofa with his long legs spilling over two additional chairs. In this position he read newspapers aloud, so as to bring two senses into play at once, and prepared his law briefs. I also visited the Lincoln tomb, a repelling shrine where a voice kept rasping over loudspeakers, "*Shh!* This is Lincoln's tomb. *Shh!*"

It was almost as bad at the White House in Washington, which I visited at the time Watergate was getting into the headlines. Borne along by noisy crowds, I was allowed to visit only a few of the rooms on the first floor. No chance to get a feel for Lincoln here.

But Ford's Theater was another matter. It has been so thoroughly restored that it looks now just as it did that Good Friday of 1865, when Lincoln came here for the last time. I sat down in one of the seats and gazed at the stage and the state box that overlooked it, trying to envision what it was like to be here on that grim and terrible night. Then across the street to the Petersen House and down to the dim little room where the doctors carried Lincoln after Booth had shot him. When I saw the four-poster bed where they lay Lincoln down, that night of nights came rushing forward—or I went hurtling back—and I could see the doctors laboring at Lincoln's side, could see Charles Sumner taking Lincoln's hand and bowing his head in tears, could hear Mary sobbing hysterically in the front parlor, while outside men and women, black people and white, waited in the rain as the president died.

When I wrote *With Malice toward None* and narrated the assassination, my visit to Ford's Theater and the Petersen House helped as much as all my research to make the final scenes live again. And when Lincoln died in my story, I could scarcely go on. I had lived with him so long, been so involved in his work and his life, come to understand so much about him, that I felt as though I had lost a member of my family. After I placed his coffin on the funeral train and sent him and Willie home together, I left my study and stumbled downstairs stricken with grief, unable to believe or to bear what had happened. And I cried.

For me, biography has not only been high literary and historical adventure, but deep personal experience as well. I have lived through three human lives besides my own, something that has enriched me immeasurably as a writer and as a man. Too, examining the impact which Turner, Brown, and Lincoln had on the America of their day has given me invaluable insights into slavery and the Civil War.

Most important, the experience of writing the trilogy reinforced my lifelong conviction that the people who inhabit the landscape of the past have never died. For me, they never will.

REFERENCES

One. Styron's War against the Blacks

This essay first appeared in *The Nation* (May 31, 1975), 662–64, under the title of "Styron & the Blacks—Another View," and is reprinted here by permission of the editors of that periodical.

Though most white reviewers were entranced with Styron's novel, there were a few who expressed reservations. For example, see Herbert Aptheker's essay in *The Nation* (October 16, 1967), 375–76. Genovese's remarks about *Ten Black Writers Respond* are from his review, "The Nat Turner Case," *New York Review of Books* (September 12, 1968), 34–37. Duberman's reviews of Styron's novel and *Ten Black Writers Respond* are collected, with italicized explanations, in Duberman's *The Uncompleted Past* (New York, 1969), 203–22.

For extensive criticisms, defenses, and refutations of Styron's novel, consult John B. Duff and Peter M. Mitchell, eds., *The Nat Turner Rebellion: The Historical Event and the Modern Controversy* (New York, 1971). Henry Irving Tragle, ed., *The Southampton Slave Revolt of 1831* (Amherst, Mass., 1971), is the best collection of documents, although Eric Foner, ed., *Nat Turner* (Englewood Cliffs, N.J., 1971), is also useful. Though crudely published, F. Roy Johnson, *The Nat Turner Slave Insurrection* (Murfreesboro, N.C., 1966), and *The Nat Turner Story* (Murfreesboro, N.C., 1970), are valuable for Southern folklore about Turner.

Two. God's Stone in the Pool of Slavery

The opening portrait of Brown and Harpers Ferry is based on my own work, *To Purge This Land with Blood: A Biography of John Brown* (New York, 1970). But I have also benefited from Professor Ronald Story's illuminating unpublished paper, "John Brown and the Injuries of Class." For recent interpretations of Brown that differ from my own, see Jules Abels, *Man on Fire* (New York, 1971), and Richard Boyer, *The Legend of John Brown* (New York, 1973).

Biographers and historians have overemphasized the abolitionist and antislavery reaction to Brown's raid and have given too little attention to the mass of conservative Northern response to that event. For a more balanced survey of Northern opinion, see Betty L. Mitchell, "Massachusetts Reacts to John Brown's Raid," *Civil War History* 19 (March 1973), 65–79; Stuart Davis, "Liberty Before Union: Massachusetts and the Coming of the Civil War" (Ph.D. dissertation, University of Massachusetts, Amherst, 1975), 37–71; and John Michael Ray, "Rhode Island Reacts to John Brown's Raid," *Rhode Island History* 20 (October 1961), 97–108. My quotation ("raid of twenty-two men") is from Allan Nevins, *The Emergence of Lincoln* (2 vols., New York, 1950), 2: 85; my quotation ("in the grand tragedy"), from *De Bow's Review* 28 (January and May 1860), 542–49.

My account of racial slavery and the Old South draws from Gerald W. Mullin, *Flight and Rebellion: Slave Resistance in Eighteenth-Century Virginia* (New York, 1972); Herbert Aptheker, *American Negro Slave Revolts* (new ed., New York, 1969); Staughton Lynd, *Class Conflict, Slavery, and the United States Constitution* (Indianapolis, Ind., 1967), 153–83; Robert McColley, *Slavery and Jeffersonian Virginia* (Urbana, Ill., 1964), 114–32; and Eugene D. Genovese, *Roll, Jordan, Roll: The World the Slaves Made* (New York, 1974), which is less a coherent narrative than a huge collection of loosely organized articles about all aspects of slavery and slave life. I have also learned a great deal about the racial nature of slavery from Winthrop D. Jordan's *White Over Black: American Attitudes toward the Negro, 1550–1812* (paperback ed., Baltimore, 1969); W. J. Cash's *The Mind of the South* (New York, 1941), 3–102; and U. B. Phillips, *The Course of the South to Secession* (reprint ed., New York, 1964), which stresses the role of slavery as a means of race control. William W. Freehling, "The Founding Fathers and Slavery," *American Historical Review* 77 (February 1972), 81–92, is instructive, although I question Freehling's contention that the Founding Fathers avoided slavery where it was volatile and restricted it where it was not. This may be true of Thomas Jefferson. But it was not true of those slaveowners who attended the Philadelphia Convention of 1787 and proved themselves absolutely unwilling to compromise on slavery inside the country.

For the great Southern reaction of the 1830s and 1840s, see Freehling, *Prelude to Civil War: The Nullification Controversy in South Carolina, 1816–1836* (New York, 1966); George M. Fredrickson, *The Black Image in the White Mind* (New York, 1971), 43–70; Clement Eaton, *Freedom-of-Thought Struggle in the Old South* (revised and enlarged ed., New York, 1964), 89*ff.*; and John Hope Franklin, *The Militant South* (Cambridge, Mass., 1966), 70–95. Calhoun's quotation ("a good—a positive good") is in Eric L. McKitrick, ed., *Slavery Defended* (Englewood Cliffs, N.J., 1963), 12–16. For Fitzhugh, see his *Sociology for the South; or the Failure of Free Society* (Richmond, 1854), 222, and Eugene D. Genovese, *The World the Slaveholders Made* (paperback ed., New York, 1971), 118–244.

My account of Southern opinion in the 1850s draws from the following modern studies: Michael Davis, *The Image of Lincoln in the South* (Knoxville, 1971), 7–61; Donald E. Reynolds, *Editors Make War: Southern Newspapers and the Secession Crisis* (Nashville, 1970); Steven A. Channing, *Crisis of Fear: Secession in South Carolina* (New York, 1970); Franklin, *The Militant South*, 96–128; Clement Eaton, *Jefferson Davis* (New York, 1977), 99–111; and especially Marshall J. Rachleff, "Racial Fear and Political Factionalism: A Study of the Secession Movement in Alabama" (Ph.D. dissertation, University of Massachusetts, Amherst, 1974). The quotation ("I shudder to contemplate it") is from the *Southern Advocate*, December 12, 1860. There were, of course, dissenters in the militant South and liberating cracks in the slave regime down to the Civil War, as shown in Carl N. Degler, *The Other South: Southern Dissenters in the Nineteenth Century* (New York, 1974), 13–157, and in Richard C. Wade, *Slavery in the Cities* (New York, 1964).

My quotations on the Southern response to Harpers Ferry are from the following sources: ("has advanced the cause of disunion") in the Richmond *Enquirer*, October 25, 1859; ("I have said of Mr. Seward") in Oswald Garrison Villard, *John Brown, 1800–1859: A Biography Fifty Years After* (New York, 1943), 506–7. Also see Rachleff and Channing as cited in the preceding paragraph and Nevins, *Emergence of Lincoln* 2, 102–31; C. Vann Woodward, "John Brown's Private War," *The Burden of Southern History* (Baton Rouge, La., 1960), 63–67; and David Brion Davis, *The Slave Power Conspiracy and the Paranoid Style* (Baton Rouge, La., 1969), 32–61. The Lincoln quotations are from Abraham Lincoln, *Collected Works* (ed. Roy P. Basler and others, 9 vols., New Brunswick, N.J., 1953–1955), 3: 538; 4: 160–61, 215–16. The quotation from the Montgomery *Mail* was reprinted in the Nashville *Banner*, November 11, 1860. Whether the Republican party in 1860 posed an immediate threat to the slave-based South is a moot issue which may never be resolved. For their part, Eric Foner, *Free Soil, Free Labor, Free Men: The Ideology of the Republican Party Before the Civil War* (New York, 1970), especially 315–17, and William W. Freehling, "Paranoia and American History," *New York Review of Books* (September 23, 1971), 36–39, contend that the Republicans in 1860 were indeed a real threat to the South and its slave system.

Three. John Brown and His Judges

This essay originally appeared, with extensive documentation, in *Civil War History* 17 (March 1971), 5–24, and I am indebted to that journal for permission to republish it. I wrote the last section specifically for this volume.

There are, of course, exceptions to the didactic literature about Brown. Mary Land's "John Brown's Ohio Environment," *Ohio State Archaeological and Historical Quarterly* 57 (January 1948), 24–47, shows how Brown was influenced by the antislavery controversies that raged in Ohio's Western Reserve and concludes that Brown was not an insane fanatic but an extreme product of that intensely antislavery region. Woodward's "John Brown's Private War," in *The Burden of Southern History*, 41–68, provides a trenchant analysis of the impact of Harpers Ferry on the South, but is marred by the author's acceptance of controversial documents regarding Brown's alleged insanity at their face value. David M. Potter's "John Brown and the Paradox of Leadership among American Negroes," in *The South and the Sectional Conflict* (Baton Rouge, La., 1968), 201–18, includes a fair appraisal of Brown's relationship with Negro leaders like Frederick Douglass, although the essay ignores the influence of Brown's religious beliefs on the Harpers Ferry attack. Boyd B. Stutler's "Abraham Lincoln and John Brown—A Parallel," *Civil War History* 8 (September 1962), is a thoughtful essay. Benjamin Quarles's *Allies for Freedom: Blacks and John Brown* (New York, 1974), is a lucid, even-tempered examination of Brown's ties with the antebellum black community and of Brown's legacy among black Americans from Harpers Ferry to our own time. And Jeffery Stuart Rossbach's "The Secret Six: A Study of the Conspiracy behind John Brown's Raid" (Ph.D. dissertation, University of Massachusetts, Amherst, 1974), is a rich and subtle discussion of why six well-educated and reasonably well-established American reformers embraced violence to solve the slavery problem.

Albert Fried's *John Brown's Journey: Notes and Reflections on His America and Mine* (New York, 1978) is the most recent sympathetic treatment of Brown himself. From what I can gather, Fried contracted in 1968 to do an actual biography of Brown, but then abandoned the project for reasons that are not clear. Several years later, after my own biography and four other studies of Brown had appeared, Fried returned to his notes and produced *John Brown's America*, an account of the time he spent in 1967–68, doing background reading on Brown in the New York Public Library. Written in the manner of a journal, the volume consists of Fried's reactions to previous writings about Brown and the author's own speculations on the man and his world, all interwoven with passages on the turmoil (the ghetto riots, the Vietnam War) of Fried's time. So far as Harpers Ferry is concerned, Fried contends that Brown planned to function as a "guerrilla provocateur" in the South, intending "not so much to create a slave revolt as generate a cycle of provocations and retaliations leading to sectional warfare and through sectional warfare, emancipation" (pp. 208–9). As I have tried to demonstrate in the text, Brown did indeed hope to foment a sectional crisis, and he thought his raid would do that whether it succeeded or failed. But there can be no doubt that he planned to incite a massive slave rebellion throughout Dixie and that he relied on Providential interposition to determine the outcome. Fried errs in dismissing this side of Harpers Ferry and assigning a single, political and ideological purpose for Brown's attack. What is more, Fried relies much too much on Villard for his factual information. As a consequence, Fried mistakenly claims (as Villard did) that Brown had perfected his Harpers Ferry enterprise by 1855, before he went to Kansas, and Fried cites as evidence Brown's notebook entries on guerrilla warfare and on Southern communities containing federal forts or arsenals. As I point out in my critique of Villard, Brown recorded these entries, not in 1855, but in the summer of 1857, after his Kansas experiences had convinced him that he must fight slavery in the South itself. Thus, Fried is completely wrong about the origins of Harpers Ferry—an error he could have avoided had he examined Brown's notebooks himself or read *To Purge This Land with Blood*, 213–14, 397. Still, Fried is fair and empathetic toward Brown himself, and he draws an especially sensitive portrait of Brown's early years as a Calvinist businessman. Unlike Malin, Nevins, and most other historians who have written about Brown, Fried has tried to understand the man, not vilify him.

One of the major themes of my own essay is the tremendous influence that Brown's Calvinist convictions had on his life and his Harpers Ferry scheme. On this point, one could cite Brown's letters almost at random, but see especially Brown to his father, June 12, 1830, John Brown Papers, Ohio Historical Society; Brown to John Jr., September 25, 1843, John Brown Letters, Illinois State Historical Library; Brown to John Jr., August 26, 1853, and Brown's Notes for a Sermon in the Boyd B. Stutler Collection, Charleston, West Virginia. See also James Foreman to James Redpath, December 28, 1859, Richard Hinton Papers, Kansas State Historical Society; George B. Delamater, address about John Brown given at Meadville, Pennsylvania, sometime after Brown's death, MS, Stutler Collection; statements of John Brown, Jr., and Ruth Brown Thompson in Franklin B. Sanborn, *Life and Letters of John Brown* (Boston, 1885), 91–95; and George B. Gill, Reminiscences, MS, Hinton Papers, Kansas State Historical Society.

In my discussion of Malin's *John Brown and the Legend of Fifty-Six*, I refer to two letters that John Jr. wrote his father and that altered Brown's reasons for going to the Kansas Territory. The letter of June 22, 1855, is in the John Brown Papers, Kansas State Historical Society; that of June 29, 1855, in the Franklin B. Sanborn Folder, Houghton Library, Harvard University.

As for the Pottawatomie massacre, I find the evidence quite convincing that Brown chose his victims because they had actively aided Missouri intruders or threatened their free-state neighbors. In fact, Brown and his self-styled "Northern Army" asked both James Harris and another man at Harris's cabin whether they had ever assisted proslavery intruders, participated in "the last troubles at Lawrence," or ever harmed or intended harm to the free-state party. They obviously answered no on all counts because Brown spared them both. Surely the old man used the same criteria in determining the fate of his actual victims. (See Harris's affidavit, June 6, 1856, "Howard Report," *U.S. House Committee Reports*, 34th Cong. 1st sess., 1855–1856, vol. 2, no. 200, p. 1179.) Numerous free-state settlers asserted shortly after the massacre that the victims, all of them connected with the proslavery court and the proslavery party, had thrown out threats and insults at their free-state neighbors. There is no contemporary evidence, however, that the victims had actually done violence to their free-state opponents, as Villard asserted.

In my essay, I argue that the retaliatory blow thesis is the best explanation for the Pottawatomie murders. Various other reasons have been given, among them: (1) that free-state leaders conceived the massacre and Brown merely executed it; (2) that Brown had reason to kill his victims because they had actually done violence to free-state settlers; (3) that he learned they were part of a conspiracy to exterminate their free-state neighbors and that Brown killed them to prevent them from doing so. For lack of convincing corroborative evidence, I have rejected these explanations.

In my discussion of Allan Nevins, the quotation ("stone in the historians' shoe") is from Truman Nelson, "John Brown Revisited," *The Nation* (August 31, 1957), 88; the quotation ("psychology and psychoanalysis have thrust") from Kendall, *The Art of Biography* (New York, 1965), 121; and the quotations about Frederick Brown's troubles from Samuel Adair, "Life of Frederick Brown," MS, Kansas Collection, University of Kansas. The affidavits about Brown's alleged insanity are located in the John Brown Papers, Library of Congress. My profile of Brown's complex personality draws from *To Purge This Land with Blood*. The quotations in the epilogue about the National Endowment for the Humanities and the Brown project are from John H. Barcroft, Director of Public Programs, to Senator Jennings Randolph, March 19, 1975, photocopy in my possession.

Four. Modern Radicals and John Brown

This essay was first published, in somewhat different form, in *The South Atlantic Quarterly* 73 (Autumn, 1974), 417–27, under the title of " 'In Thine Own Image': Modern Radicals and John Brown," and I thank the *Quarterly* for permission to reprint the piece.

Louis Ruchames's conception of Brown appears in his anthology of documents, *John Brown: The Making of a Revolutionary* (reprint of the 1959 ed., New York, 1969), 18, 23, 39–40. See also Ruchames's exchange with Willie Lee Rose in the *New York Review of Books* (February 11, 1971), 43–44. Aptheker discussed Brown and Du Bois's *John Brown* (Philadelphia, 1909) during a series of lectures on Du Bois's life and work, delivered at the University of Massachusetts, Amherst, from September 22, 1971, to May 11, 1972.

The fullest expression of Nelson's interpretation of Brown appears in his book, *The Old Man* (New York, 1973), which contends that Harpers Ferry must be viewed as a partisan coup rather than an attempted insurrection. For a discussion of Brown's Calvinism and growing antislavery militancy, along with annotated citations to the sources, consult *To Purge This Land with Blood*. See also the excellent selection of Brown letters in Ruchames, *John Brown*, 43–167, and the many letters and documents in Villard's *John Brown*, a biography which Nelson admires.

My discussion of Brown's objectives at Harpers Ferry derives from Salmon's statement in Villard, *John Brown*, 56; Gerrit Smith's letter of August 27, 1859, to the "Jerry Anniversary Committee," in Ralph V. Harlow, *Gerrit Smith* (New York, 1939), 405–6; Franklin Preston Stearns, *George Luther Stearns* (Philadelphia, 1907), 164; Villard, *John Brown*, 324; Gerrit Smith to Joshua Giddings, March 25, 1858, in the Giddings Papers, Ohio Historical Society, Columbus; documents pertaining to the Chatham Convention and to Brown's expectations of widespread slave support from all over the South, in the "Mason Report," *U.S. Senate Committee Reports, 1859–1860*, 2: 1–12, 45*ff*; John Brown's Notebooks 2, Boston Public Library; description of Brown's Southern maps in the *New York Times*, October 22, 1859; Leeman's letter to his mother, September 9, 1859, in the Richard J. Hinton Papers, Kansas State Historical Society, Topeka; and Brown's statements to Sanborn, Stearns, Hanway, and Emerson, cited in Oates, *To Purge This Land with Blood*, 197, 258, 395. For a brilliant analysis of how other leftists have misunderstood and misrepresented such figures as Booker T. Washington, Du Bois, Marcus Garvey, and Malcolm X, see Harold Cruse, *Rebellion and Revolution* (New York, 1968), 193–258.

Five. The Enigma of Stephen A. Douglas

This essay first appeared in *Reviews in American History* (December 1973), 1: 534–41, under the title of "The Little Giant Reconsidered," and I thank Stanley I. Kutler, editor of that journal, for permission to republish it. I added the discussion of why the Republicans refused to compromise during the secession winter of 1860–1861.

The quotation ("lashed himself") is from John Quincy Adams, *Memoirs* (12

vols., Philadelphia, 1874–1877), 11: 510–11. Allan Nevins elaborated on his interpretation of the Kansas-Nebraska Act in his essay, "The Constitution, Slavery,
and the Territories," in *The Gaspar G. Bacon Lectures on the Constitution of
the United States, 1940–1950* (Boston, 1953), 97–141. While Johannsen's *Douglas*
is a source book in itself, see also Robert W. Johannsen, ed., *The Letters of
Stephen A. Douglas* (Urbana, Ill., 1961).

The standard work on the Republicans and secession is David M. Potter's
Lincoln and His Party in the Secession Crisis (New Haven, 1942). But see also
Potter's *The Impending Crisis, 1848–1861* (completed and edited by Don E.
Fehrenbacher, New York, 1976), 405–583, and Kenneth M. Stampp, *And the War
Came: The North and the Secession Crisis, 1860–1861* (paperback ed., Chicago,
1964). Davis's "Liberty Before Union: Massachusetts and the Coming of the Civil
War" is an excellent analysis of a crucial Union state during the secession crisis.

Six. Lincoln's Journey to Emancipation

This essay was originally an address I gave in the Chancellor's Lecture Series,
February 5, 1976, at the University of Massachusetts, Amherst. I substantially
revised the essay for publication here.

For the growth of Lincoln mythology, see Richard N. Current, *The Lincoln
Nobody Knows* (New York, 1958), 266–87, and Lloyd Lewis, *Myths After Lincoln*
(New York, 1929). Roy P. Basler, *The Lincoln Legend* (Boston, 1935), stresses the
literary uses of the myths, whereas David Donald, *Lincoln Reconsidered* (New
York, 1956), 3–18, and Alfred H. Jones, *Roosevelt's Image Brokers: Poets, Play-
wrights, and the Use of the Lincoln Symbol* (Port Washington, N.Y., 1974),
examine the political uses of the myths.

My profile of Lincoln as a man is based on the following sources: quotation
("the most miserable man living") in Lincoln, *Collected Works*, 1: 229; Lincoln's
letters to Speed about their romantic troubles, ibid., 259–61, 265–66, 267–68,
269–70, 280–81, 282, 288–89; Lincoln and Mary Todd in Justin G. and Linda
Levitt Turner, eds., *Mary Todd Lincoln, Her Life and Letters* (New York, 1972),
23–34, and Ruth Painter Randall, *Mary Lincoln, Biography of a Marriage* (Boston, 1953), 65–85; Lincoln and Matthew Gentry in Lincoln, *Collected Works*,
1: 368–70, 385–86; Lincoln and liquor, Albert J. Beveridge, *Abraham Lincoln,
1809–1858* (2 vols., Boston, 1928), 1: 82–83, 534; quotation ("all conquering mind")
in Lincoln, *Collected Works*, 1: 279; Lincoln's humor, Henry C. Whitney, *Life
on the Circuit with Lincoln* (Boston, 1892), 171; Lincoln's story, "Bass-Ackwards," in Lincoln, *Collected Works*, 8: 420; Lincoln and his father, ibid., 4: 61;
Lincoln's finances, Harry E. Pratt, *The Personal Finances of Abraham Lincoln*
(Springfield, Ill., 1943); Herndon's quotation on the Irish in his article in the
New York Tribune, February 15, 1867; Lincoln and the Declaration of Independence, Lincoln, *Collected Works*, 2: 266; 4: 168–69, 235–36, 240.

Lincoln's views on slavery before 1854: Lincoln, *Collected Works*, 1: 74–75; 2:
230–83, 492; 4: 65; quotation ("making me miserable") ibid., 1: 260; 2: 320;
quotation ("sort of Negro livery stable") ibid., 2: 237–238, 253; quotation ("glorious consummation") ibid., 132.

For Lincoln's reactions to the Kansas-Nebraska Act, see the speeches in ibid.,

2: 247–83, 398–410. Lincoln's celebrated "House Divided" speech, ibid., 461–69, outlines the stages of the Slave-Power conspiracy as Lincoln saw it; but see also ibid., 2: 341; 3: 53–54, 204–5.

My own work, *With Malice toward None: The Life of Abraham Lincoln* (New York, 1977), 149–60, narrates the Lincoln-Douglas debates from Lincoln's point of view, whereas Johannsen's *Douglas*, 641–79, relates them from Douglas's perspective. The speeches of both men are gathered in Lincoln, *Collected Works*, vols. 2 and 3, and in Paul M. Angel, ed., *Created Equal? The Complete Lincoln-Douglas Debates of 1858* (Chicago, 1958). My discussion of Lincoln's views on Negroes draws from Lincoln, *Collected Works* 2: 405, 501; 3: 16–30, 145–46; and 5: 372–73. For an analysis of Lincoln in the 1850s, see Don E. Fehrenbacher, *Prelude to Greatness* (Stanford, Ca., 1962).

For Lincoln and the South, see Lincoln, *Collected Works* 3: 204–5, 374–75, 522–50, and Davis, *Image of Lincoln in the South*, 7–40. My quotation ("the South, the loyal South") comes from the Atlanta *Southern Confederacy* as reprinted in the *New York Times*, August 7, 1860.

For the pressures on Lincoln to free the slaves, consult David Donald, *Charles Sumner and the Rights of Man* (New York, 1970), 22 ff., and my article, "Death Warrant for Slavery," *American Heritage*, forthcoming. Also informative are Hans L. Trefousse, *The Radical Republicans, Lincoln's Vanguard for Racial Justice* (New York, 1969), 171–73, 203–22; George Washington Julian, *Political Recollections, 1840–1872* (Chicago, 1884); Patrick W. Riddleberger, *George Washington Julian, Radical Republican* (Indianapolis, 1966); the Detroit *Post and Tribune, Zachariah Chandler* (Detroit, 1880); Fawn M. Brodie, *Thaddeus Stevens, Scourge of the South* (paperback ed., New York, 1966); and Edward Magdol, *Owen Lovejoy, Abolitionist in Congress* (New Brunswick, N.J., 1967). For Lincoln's gradual emancipation plan, see Lincoln, *Collected Works* 5: 145–46, 317–19, and Charles M. Segal, ed., *Conversations with Lincoln* (New York, 1961), 165–68. My quotation ("strong hand on the colored element") is from Lincoln, *Collected Works* 7: 281–82.

Gideon Welles, "History of Emancipation," *Galaxy* (December 1872), 842–43, and Welles, *Diary* (ed. John T. Morse, Jr., 3 vols., Boston, 1911), 1: 70–71, describe the carriage ride in which Lincoln discussed emancipation. The first draft of the preliminary Emancipation Proclamation is in Lincoln, *Collected Works* 5: 336–37. My quotation ("our last shriek") is from Glyndon G. Van Deusen, *William Henry Seward* (New York, 1967), 331. For a discussion of emancipation and Lincoln's message to Congress, December 1862, see *With Malice toward None*, 325–26. The final Proclamation is in Lincoln, *Collected Works*, 6: 28–30. The quotation ("my name") is from Segal, *Conversations with Lincoln*, 234–35; the quotation ("time of times") from James M. McPherson, ed., *The Negro's Civil War* (New York, 1965), 50. See also John Hope Franklin, *The Emancipation Proclamation* (Garden City, N.Y., 1965).

As is clear from the text, I do not agree with Richard Hofstadter's view in *The American Political Tradition and the Men Who Made It* (New York, 1948), 131, that Lincoln's Proclamation "added nothing to what Congress had already done in the [Second] Confiscation Act" and that "it did not in fact free any slaves," since it applied only to rebel states where Lincoln had no control. Though hugely popular both in and out of the academies, this is an erroneous and really quite preposterous argument. By war's end, Lincoln's Proclamation had uprooted slavery as an institution and emancipated hundreds of thousands of blacks in conquered and occupied Dixie. To say that Lincoln's Proclamation—a declaration of war against slavery—broke no slave chains in the rebel South is rather like claiming that Franklin D. Roosevelt's War Message and Congress's War Declaration of December 8, 1941, did not in fact kill any Japanese, since on that day the documents applied only to a people beyond Roosevelt's control.

The best studies of Lincoln and black troops are Dudley T. Cornish, *The Sable Arm: Negro Troops in the Union Army, 1861–1865* (paperback ed., New York, 1966), and Benjamin Quarles, *The Negro in the Civil War* (Boston, 1953). The Lincoln quotations ("the great *available* . . . force" and "with clenched teeth") are from Lincoln, *Collected Works*, 6: 149–50, 410.

V. Jacque Voegeli, *Free But Not Equal: The Midwest and the Negro during the Civil War* (Chicago, 1967), 95–112, has an excellent discussion of the Union refugee program. Also useful are Benjamin Quarles, *Lincoln and the Negro* (New York, 1962), 188–90, and Bell. I. Wiley, *Southern Negroes, 1861–1865* (paperback ed., Baton Rouge, La., 1965), 199–259. As for Lincoln's views on colonization and Negro rights, I sharply disagree with George M. Fredrickson, who, in "A Man But Not a Brother: Abraham Lincoln and Racial Equality," *Journal of Southern History* 41 (February 1975), 39–58, argues that Lincoln continued "to his dying day to deny the possibility of racial harmony and equality in the United States and persisted in regarding colonization as the only real alternative to perpetual race conflict." As evidence for this, Fredrickson cites only Benjamin Butler's recollection, as given in *Butler's Book* (Boston, 1892), that Lincoln in April 1865 still feared a race war in the South and still wanted to colonize all blacks abroad. Not only is Butler a questionable witness, but there is not a shred of corroborative evidence for the position he attributed to Lincoln, not another single source that quoted the president, in public or in private, as saying that he still wanted to ship the blacks out of the country. What is more, Butler's remarks—and Fredrickson's contention based on them—contradict Lincoln's own race and reconstruction policies that I outline further on in my essay. Finally, Fredrickson's entire argument on this matter ignores Lincoln's tremendous capacity for growth and change, something I have tried to demonstrate.

On the reaction to Lincoln's Proclamation, the quotation ("brink of ruin") is from Orville H. Browning, *Diary* (ed. Theodore Calvin Pease and James G. Randall, 2 vols., Springfield, Ill., 1927–1933), 1: 610–13, 616; the quotation ("a coarse, but an expressive figure") from Lincoln, *Collected Works*, 6: 48–49; the quotation ("mind acts slowly") from Magdol, *Owen Lovejoy*, 401. Lincoln's abortive peace proposal to Jefferson Davis is in Lincoln, *Collected Works*, 7: 517–18; see also John G. Nicolay and John Hay, *Abraham Lincoln, A History* (10 vols., N.Y., 1890), 9: 221.

For Lincoln and the Thirteenth Amendment, see Albert G. Riddle, *Recollections of War Time* (New York, 1895), 323–24, and Julian, *Political Recollections*, 250. The quotation ("greatest measure") is from Brodie, *Stevens*, 204; the quotation ("born with a new life") from Julian, *Political Recollections*, 251; the quotations ("moral victory" and "King's cure") from Lincoln, *Collected Works*, 8: 254–55; the quotation ("people over the river") from Segal, *Conversations with Lincoln*, 17

Lincoln's Second Inaugural and his speech of April 11, 1865, are in Lincoln, *Collected Works*, 8: 332–33, 399–405. For discussions of Lincoln's military approach to reconstruction, consult Donald, *Charles Sumner and the Rights of Man*, 196–207; Benjamin Thomas and Harold M. Hyman, *Stanton, The Life and Times of Lincoln's Secretary of War* (New York, 1962), 357–58; and Oates, *With Malice toward None*, 369–71, 377–79, 406–7, 423–25, 427–28.

For Lincoln and Frederick Douglass, see Douglass's article in the *New York Tribune*, July 15, 1885, and Douglass, *Life and Times* (reprint of revised 1892 ed., New York, 1962), 347–49, 484–86. The closing quotation is from Lincoln, *Collected Works*, 5: 537.

Seven. The Long Shadow of Lincoln

The books discussed in this essay—Mitgang's anthology, *Abraham Lincoln, A Press Portrait* (Chicago, 1971), Dicey's *Spectator of America* (ed. Herbert Mitgang, Chicago, 1971), and Brooks's *Washington, D.C., in Lincoln's Time* (ed. Herbert Mitgang, Chicago, 1971)—are handsome reprint editions, offered by Quadrangle as a trilogy called *Lincoln's Long Shadow*. Brooks's celebrated volume and Mitgang's press portrait were first published in 1895 and 1956, respectively. And Dicey's superb travel account originally appeared in England in 1863, under the title of *Six Months in the Federal States*. My essay grew out of a review of the trilogy that I published in *Civil War History* 18 (September 1972), 251–54.

There are a number of other excellent contemporary accounts of Lincoln and the war. John Hay's *Lincoln and the Civil War in the Diaries and Letters of John Hay* (ed. Tyler Dennett, reprint ed., Westport, Conn., 1972) is filled with eyewitness descriptions of people and happenings in wartime Washington. I have learned a great deal from William Howard ("Bull Run") Russell's *My Diary, North and South* (reprint ed., ed. Fletcher Pratt, New York, 1954), and have benefited from Welles's *Diary* and Salmon Chase's *Inside Lincoln's Cabinet: The Civil War Diaries of Salmon P. Chase* (ed. David Donald, New York, 1954). Browning's *Diary* is also informative, though it must be used with care since Browning tended to make his own conservative opinions those of Lincoln as well. Segal's *Conversations with Lincoln* is a superlative collection of interviews. And F. B. Carpenter, *Six Months at the White House with Lincoln* (Century House edition, ed. John Crosby Freeman, Watkins Glen, N.Y., 1961), is a vivid human portrait by the man who painted *The First Reading of the Emancipation Proclamation*, which now hangs in the Capitol. Elizabeth Keckley's *Behind the Scenes: Thirty Years a Slave and Four Years in the White House* (reprint ed., New York, 1968) is a valuable and revealing document written by Mary Lincoln's intelligent and compassionate seamstress. The authenticity of Keckley's book has often been questioned, though, because journalist James Redpath may have helped her write it. Still, Keckley was an honest woman who set out to tell the truth, and I cannot believe that she would allow distortions or prevarications to mar her book. Moreover, many of her stories can be corroborated by other eyewitness accounts.

Eight. *Carl Sandburg's Lincoln*

This essay grew out of a paper I wrote for a symposium on Carl Sandburg as a Lincoln biographer, held on January 21, 1978, at Knox College in Galesburg, Illinois. Historian Robert W. Johannsen, Congressman Paul Simon of Illinois, and biographer Justin Kaplan also contributed papers to the symposium. My opening passages are based on the following sources: quotations ("I think the Lincoln book," "I look at this damned vast manuscript," and "Sibelius bleakness") from Herbert Mitgang, ed., *The Letters of Carl Sandburg* (New York, 1968), 221, 363, 367, 373; quotation ("this has grown into a scroll") from North Callahan, *Carl Sandburg, Lincoln of Our Literature* (New York, 1970), 119; the Quaife quotation from Benjamin P. Thomas, *Portrait for Posterity: Lincoln and His Biographers* (New Brunswick, N.J., 1947), 285, 286, 301; the Hofstadter quotation from Hofstadter, *The American Political Tradition and the Men Who Made It* (New York, 1948), 360; the Wilson quotation from Wilson, *Patriotic Gore: Studies in the Literature of the American Civil War* (New York, 1962), 115; the Benét quotation from the *Atlantic Monthly* (December 1939), 22; the Sherwood quotation from the *New York Times Book Review*, December 5, 1939; the Callahan quotation from Callahan, *Sandburg*, 139; the Donald quotation from the *New York Times Book Review*, March 13, 1977; and the Thomas quotation from Thomas, *Portrait for Posterity*, 310. Sandburg so loved Thomas's remark that he quoted it in *Abraham Lincoln: The Prairie Years and the War Years* (one-volume ed., New York, 1954), 747.

My argument for true biography draws heavily from Kendall's brilliant and indispensable book, *The Art of Biography* (New York, 1965), ix, 15, 17, 21–23, 28, 113–53. Though I do not agree with everything said in them, I have also learned much about biography from Catherine Drinker Bowen, *Biography: The Craft and the Calling* (Boston, 1969); Richard D. Altick, *Lives and Letters: A History of Literary Biography in England and America* (New York, 1969); and John A. Garraty, *The Nature of Biography* (New York, 1957).

The sources for my critique of Sandburg's *Abraham Lincoln: The Prairie Years* (2 vols., New York, N.Y., 1926), are as follows: Sandburg's quotation about Lucy and Nancy Hanks, his folk tales about young Lincoln, and his quotations about Lincoln and Ann Rutledge, all from *Lincoln, The Prairie Years*, 1: 12, 50, 51–52, 73, 138, 140–41, 189–90 (see also 16, 33, 40, 41–42, 43, 56–59, 71ff., 187, and 290 for other fictional passages); the Wilson quotation in *Patriotic Gore*, 116; Sandburg, *Lincoln* (one-volume ed.), 38–40, 45–46; quotation ("a son of the prairie") from Callahan, *Sandburg*, 101; quotations ("stubby, homely words," "the Strange Friend," "like something out of a picture book for children," and "a mind, a spirit, a tongue") from Sandburg, *Lincoln: The Prairie Years*, 2: 105, 284, 428, and 1: 480; quotation ("fabulous human figure") from Sandburg, *Lincoln* (one-volume ed.), 296. In *Lincoln: The Prairie Years*, 2: 105, Sandburg falsely describes as "a homely and almost friendly declaration" Lincoln's serious allegation in the House Divided speech that Douglas, Pierce, Taney, and Buchanan were part of a Slave-Power plot to nationalize slavery. Moreover, in his account of the Freeport debate in 1858, Sandburg repeats an enduring error that Lincoln was out to ruin Douglas's presidential chances in 1860. For a correction of that error, see Fehrenbacher, *Prelude to Greatness*, 121–41. For the truth about Lincoln and

Ann Rutledge, consult J. G. Randall, *Lincoln the President* (paperback ed., New York, 1945), 2: 321–41; David Donald, *Lincoln's Herndon* (New York, N.Y., 1948), 218–41; and the editors' note on Rutlege in Lincoln, *Collected Works*, 4: 104.

My discussion of the Lincoln not found in the *Prairie Years* derives from John J. Duff, *A. Lincoln, Prairie Lawyer* (New York, 1960), 45–46, 243–71 passim; Lincoln, *Collected Works*, 1: 94–95, 265*ff.*, 282, 367–70, 384–86, and 3: 472–73; Reinhard H. Luthin, *The Real Abraham Lincoln* (Englewood Cliffs, N.J., 1960), 123–25; Paul M. Angle, ed., *Abraham Lincoln, by Some Men Who Knew Him* (reprint ed., Freeport, N.Y., 1969), 50, 53–54, 109; Oates, *With Malice toward None*, Parts One-Six; and Charles Strozier's "The Search for Identity and Love in Young Lincoln," forthcoming. Sandburg does provide block quotations of Lincoln's poetry and his letters to Mary Owens and Joshua Speed, but makes nothing of Lincoln's fears of intimacy with women and little of his obsessions with death and madness. Furthermore, Sandburg makes only slight and fleeting references to Lincoln's important work in the Illinois Supreme Court (for instance, see the *Prairie Years*, 2: 67, 358). Worse, of course, are Sandburg's omissions about Lincoln and Negroes in the 1858 debates. He does not report a single word of Lincoln's anti-Negro remarks at Ottawa and Charleston (see Lincoln, *Collected Works*, 3: 16, 145–46). In their place, Sandburg cites Lincoln's relatively mild utterance at Springfield that "certainly the Negro is not our equal in color—perhaps not in other respects" (*Lincoln: The Prairie Years*, 2: 131). Sandburg also plays down Lincoln's remarks about blacks in his speech of June 26, 1857, quoting only an inoffensive statement that there were enough whites to marry whites and blacks to marry blacks (ibid., 95). Since Douglas persisted in race baiting Republicans, Lincoln conceded in his speech that there was "a natural disgust" among nearly all whites at the idea of racial amalgamation, and he and his party opposed it too. Still, when compared to the white-supremacist, anti-Negro attitudes of Douglas and most other white people of that time, Lincoln comes off as an enlightened man in the matter of race relations, as I have tried to demonstrate in chapter six.

The sources for my description of Sandburg, *Abraham Lincoln: The War Years* (4 vols., New York, 1939), are as follows: quotation ("events of wild passionate onrush") from ibid., vii; quotation ("both of the Lincoln who belonged to the people") from Callahan, *Sandburg,* 123; Sandburg's Lincoln as a people's hero from *Lincoln: The War Years*, 2: 562, 587, 589–92, 646, also 3: 300, 391, 567–68, and 4: 216–17; Sandburg's Lincoln, the so-called radicals, and the South and reconstruction from ibid., 4: 217, also 2: 559–60, and 3: 82, 642; quotation ("silence, grief") from ibid., 4: 350–51; Sandburg's apocryphal story about Lincoln and Mary Lincoln's loyalty in ibid., 2: 200; quotation ("You are nothing") from A. G. Frick [?] to Lincoln, February 14, 1861, Chicago Historical Society; quotation ("knew his American people") from Sandburg, *Lincoln: The War Years,* 4: 216–17.

For the unpopularity of emancipation and of Lincoln himself, consult Voegeli, *Free But Not Equal*; Forrest G. Wood, *Black Scare: The Racist Response to Emancipation and Reconstruction* (Berkeley and Los Angeles, Ca., 1968), chaps. 1–4; and the appropriate sources described above for chapter six. The quotation ("vote *against* McClellan") is from Donald, *Sumner and the Rights of Man*, 190–91. My account of Lincoln's relationship with the so-called radical Republicans draws from ibid., 12–207; Trefousse, *Radical Republicans*, chaps. 5–8; Bruce Catton, *Never Call Retreat* (Garden City, N.Y., 1965), 291–92; Thomas and Hyman, *Stanton*, 357–58; and Oates, "Death Warrant for Slavery," *American Heritage*, forthcoming. The quotation ("the eggs of crocodiles") is from Charles Sumner, *Works* (15 vols., Boston, 1870–1880), 10: 44; and the quotation ("baffling and completely inexplicable") is from Mitgang, ed., *Letters of Carl Sandburg*, 490. For an excellent discussion of myth, see Richard E. Hughes, *The Lively Image: 4 Myths in Literature* (Cambridge, Mass., 1975).

Nine. Ghost Riders in the Sky

This essay first appeared in *The Colorado Quarterly* 23 (Summer, 1974), 67–68, and I am indebted to that journal for permission to republish it. I have revised and lengthened the section on Nixon.

The Reagan quotations are from his book (written with Richard G. Hubler), *Where's the Rest of Me?* (New York, 1965), 297, 299, 302–03, 305. See also Lee Edwards, *Ronald Reagan, A Political Biography* (San Diego, Ca. 1967), 51ff. Wayne's remarks are from his interview in *Playboy Magazine* (May 1971), 80, 82, 84, 86, 88, 92.

My account of Nixon and *Chisum* is based on a report in the *New York Times*, August 4, 1970; "Richard Nixon, Moviegoer," *Newsweek* (August 17, 1970), 25; "Nixon the Crime Fighter," *The Nation* (August 17, 1970), 98–99; and Perry D. Hall, ed., *The Quotable Richard M. Nixon* (Anderson, S.C., 1967), 6, 10, 43, 49, 148–49. Earl Mazo and Stephen Hess, *Nixon. A Political Portrait* (New York, 1967), 11, 19, record Nixon's early interest in history. Nixon's lessons of the past are from Richard M. Nixon, *Six Crises* (New York, 1962), 1, 282, and Hall, *Quotable Nixon*, 11, 47, 51, 68, 86, 107, 121, 182. For other discussions of Nixon, see Fawn M. Brodie, *Presidential Sin: Jefferson to Nixon* (Davis Memorial Lecture III, Gonzaga University, Spokane, Wash., 1975), and Garry Wills, *Nixon Agonistes: The Crisis of the Self-Made Man* (Boston, 1970).

In my discussion of the real West, the quotation ("corporate, community") is from Joe B. Frantz, "The Frontier Tradition: An Invitation to Violence," in H. D. Graham and T. R. Gurr, eds., *Violence in America* (New York, 1969), 142; the quotation ("dead Indian") from Dee Brown, *Bury My Heart at Wounded Knee* (paperback ed., New York, 1972), 166.

Ten. Themes and Variations of a Civil War Trilogy

Novelists, of course, are the great masters of the art of narration, and fledgling biographers should study serious fictionists to learn the techniques of dramatic narration and character development. For a discussion of the art of historical narration, I recommend Wallace Stegner's brilliant essay, "On the Writing of History," in Stegner's *The Sound of Mountain Water* (Garden City, N.Y., 1969), 202–22. Kendall's *Art of Biography*, listed above under Sandburg's Lincoln, is a veritable manual of how to do life-writing. Bowen's *Biography: The Craft and the Calling* and André Maurois's *Aspects of Biography* (New York, 1929) are both rewarding. Justin Kaplan's "The 'Real Life,' " *Harvard English Studies* 8 (Cambridge, Mass., 1978), 1–8, is an illuminating discussion of the nature, purpose, and pitfalls of true or "literary" biography, with special reference to his new work on Walt Whitman. For a historical perspective, consult Edward H. O'Neill's *A History of American Biography, 1800–1935* (Philadelphia, 1935).

INDEX

48–49, 133; as immortal hero, 44–48; literary treatment of, 22–42; loving nature of, 39, 47–48; on necessity of war, 83; plans for invasion of South, 25–26, 48–49, 133; religious beliefs of, 24–25, 45, 46, 49–50, 133; role in Kansas civil war, 27, 33–34; sanity of, 34, 36–41; Southern view of, 72; treatment of Negroes, 39–40; view on slavery, 9–10

Brown, John, Jr., 33; letter to father, 26, 27, 31, 32; sanity of, 38

Brown, Ruth Mills, sanity of, 37

Brown, Salmon: on J. Brown's motives for Harpers Ferry, 48; sanity of, 38

Buchanan portrait, 91

Calhoun, John C., proslavery Senate speech, 16

Callahan, North, on Sandburg's *Lincoln*, 100

Caper, Gerald, *Stephen A. Douglas, Defender of the Union* (1959), 53

Cassidy, Hopalong, 114

Chamberlin, Joseph Edgar, Brown biography, bias of, 23

Chandler, Zachariah, pressure on Lincoln from, 73

Charles Sumner and the Coming of the Civil War (Donald), 41

Charleston, insurrection plots in, 14

Charleston *Mercury*, 87

Chase, Salmon, 84

Chatham (Canada) convention, 48

Chicago *Times*, 87

Chisum, 114

The Civil War and Reconstruction (Donald), 41

Clarke, John Henrik, *William Styron's Nat Turner: Ten Black Writers Respond* (1968), 1–2

Clay, Henry, 67

Colonization proposals: Lincoln and, 67–68, 75–76, 81; Virginia discussion of, 14–15

Communists, 112, 113

Confederacy, British recognition of, 74

Confessions of Nat Turner (Styron), 1–8

Confiscation act, second, 77, 108, 137

Connelley, William E., Brown biography, bias of, 23

Constitution, slavery and, 13

Craven, Avery, critique of Warren's Brown biography, 29

Crisis of the House Divided (Jaffa), 55

Crittenden resolution, Douglas support of, 53

Cruse, Harold, 7

Davis, Henry Winter, Brook's commentary on, 95

Declaration of Independence: Lincoln and, 62, 66; Southerners and, 69

Democratic party, Southern domination of, 17, 68–69

Democrats, Northern, Brown's view of, 10

Dicey, Edward: on Americans, 88, 89–90; *Spectator of America* (1971), 86, 89

Division and Reunion: America, 1848–1877 (Johnson), 41

Donald, David: *Charles Sumner and the Coming of the Civil War* (1960), 41; *The Civil War and Reconstruction* (1969), 41; on Sandburg's *Lincoln*, 100

Douglas, Stephen A., 52–60; characterization by H. Jaffa, 55–56; characterization by R.W. Johannsen, 55–60; characterization by G.F. Milton, 53–54; characterization by A. Nevins, 54–55; characterization by D. Wells, 55; Democratic party and, 56; doctrine of unfriendly legislation, 58; Freeport doctrine, 58; popular sovereignty and, 53–58; in presidential campaign of 1860, 58; Senate campaign of 1858, 70; on slavery, 53, 54, 55, 56; mention, 68

Douglass, Frederick: John Brown and, 25, 30, 31; on Lincoln, 80, 85; mention, 26, 47, 80

Dred Scott decision, 68